THE
MODERN
MAN'S
GUIDE TO
MODERN
WOMEN

THE MODERN MAN'S GUIDE TO MODERN WOMEN

Denis Boyles

HarperPerennial
A Division of HarperCollins*Publishers*

Portions of this book have appeared in *Playboy* and *Men's Health.*

HarperCollins books may be purchased for educational, business, or sales promotional use. For information please write: Special Markets Department, HarperCollins Publishers, Inc., 10 East 53rd Street, New York, NY 10022.

FIRST EDITION

Designed by Irving Perkins Associates

Library of Congress Cataloging-in-Publication Data

Boyles, Denis.
The modern man's guide to modern women / by Denis Boyles
1st ed.
p. cm.
ISBN 0–06–096899–0 (pbk.)
1. Man–woman relationships—United States. 2. Men—United
States—Psychology. 3. Women—United States—Psychology. 4. Men—United
States—Conduct of life. II. Title.
HQ801.B83 1993
305.3—dc20
92–53417

---

93 94 95 96 97 CC/RRD 10 9 8 7 6 5 4 3 2 1 (pbk.)

To
Harry Thomason and Joel Shukovsky,
Julio Iglesias and Willie Nelson.

Ye rigid Ploughmen! Bear in mind
Your labour is for future hours.
Advance! Spare not! Nor look behind!
Plough deep and straight with all your powers!
                    —RICHARD HENRY HORNE

Terence, this is stupid stuff.
                    —A. E. HOUSMAN

CONTENTS

FOREWORD

It's an unusual preface that argues against the work it introduces. But
there are some things in life better not faced head-on, and this book
contains all of them. Mind you, you hold in your hands an excellent
compendium of strategy and tactics. Mr. Boyles and his colleagues are
the Carl von Clausewitzes of the battle between the sexes. But, in a war
where every victory is Pyrrhic, what use is concentration of superior
force, flanking maneuver, diversionary thrust, or even a pincher movement on a crowded bus? And that's as if we had any victories. In those
rare engagements of gender where the man comes out, as it were, on top,
the first thing that he does is surrender.

On another front, have you ever won an argument with your mother?
She has bested you in every debate and disputation from "Resolved: We
Shall Be Weaned" to "The Case Against Asking Your First Wife to
Leave Her Drunk Second Husband in the Car at Your Daughter's
Wedding." If you can't prevail over an aged woman whose every weak-
ness and foible you know and with whom you have been contending
your entire life, how do you expect to do against a team from out of
town?

And then there is the question of whether publishing this book endan-
gers malekind. The wisdom herein contained is normally a part of masculine oral tradition. These sagacious observations are wrung from the
wet towel of interpersonal relationships by hands grown horn'ed with
the writing of child support checks. The droplets of hard-won perspicac-
ity are then passed confidentially from man to man in smoky bars,

muddy duck blinds, and country and western song lyrics. Perhaps your own dad, when you were of a suitable age, took you into his den, loaded up his pipe, looked over the top of his reading glasses, and said, "If it flies, floats, or fucks—*rent it.*"

All over the world pudgy, balding, experienced fellows are telling callow youths:

"Cookin' lasts, kissin' don't."

"They all look the same if you turn 'em upside down."

"When the groom farts in front of the bride, the honeymoon is over."

But now we have made the grave error of committing these dicta to print. They are not the sort of things men should ever put in writing. Our mothers, sisters, wives, and girlfriends (the last two, we hope, not at the same time) are going to see this book, pick it up, start reading it, and . . . laugh.

Because we don't know what we're talking about. Men don't know anything about women. We never have. We never will. Oh, each of us knows a few specific things. I, for instance, know why most societies don't allow women in combat. Combat is just a battle to the death. You don't want to turn it into something really ugly, like a marriage. But we don't know what makes women tick. Let alone shop.

We can pool our knowledge, and that is what this book sets out to do. But even then we are like the blind man trying to describe the elephant— after the elephant has moved to Boulder with its aerobics instructor. On the subject of women, I'm afraid there's nothing to say. And I, for one, don't want to be caught saying it.

This business of males and females trying to understand each other is an odd phenomenon anyway, and a recent one. Maybe we would all— men and women alike—be better off admitting our bewilderment and returning to the ignorant ways of the past. In my father's day a man married the first woman who allowed him to unclasp her brassiere. And a woman married the first man she met who had a job and didn't wipe his nose on his suit coat sleeve. Then they settled down, had children, stayed together no matter what, and were miserable, the same as us. But at least it was a peaceful, stable, unworried misery and never needed any self-help books written about it, just an occasional *Madame Bovary*.

The difficulty men have with women is really much worse than a clash of the sexes. The problem is not that 50 percent of people are females. The problem is that 100 percent of females are humans. Take a human of any kind or type, whisper nonsense to it, rub its private parts, flirt with its best friend, expect it to cook for you, and see what you get. We don't know anything about women because we don't know anything about Homo sapiens. Anyone who has studied psychology, sociology, anthropology, or any of the other wacko-and-wog disciplines knows the three great rules of the social sciences: Folks do lots of things. We don't know why. Test on Friday.

We know nothing about women. We know nothing about men. We don't even know anything about our own fool selves. (Although, if you want to find out some things about yourself—and in vivid detail, too—just try calling your wife "fat.")

There are no cures for the ills this book addresses. The author can only make a few small practical suggestions. I have one myself. Girls should be given more realistic dolls—Betsy-Wetsys that spit up, stink, and howl for hours, Barbies that sag, and Kens that lose their jobs and hair. This would result, I posit, in less distaff whining later on.

But all such recommendations are trifling—a mere cleaning of the storm drains on the continent Atlantis. The basic conundrum remains. We are in love with members of a troublesome species.

Why don't we fall for dogs? They can have as many as *eight* tits. Small ones, true, but think of it—eight! Dogs are friendly, loyal, a little jealous sometimes, but not possessed of any abstract ideas about monogamy (or anything else). They don't spend hours on the phone or put fuzzy covers on the toilet seat lid so that while you're standing there taking a leak the seat comes right back down aimed square at the principal organ of male thought. Dog jewelry is pretty much limited to a rabies vaccination tag. Dogs never want you to spend Christmas at their mother's house and can't insist on going to fancy restaurants because they aren't allowed inside. Dogs don't care if you shave and they actually like it when you leave dirty socks in the middle of the bedroom floor. Dogs do chase cars, but that's better than asking you to buy them one. And dogs never own cats.

Dogs are good-looking. Their hair is beautiful—although they have a little too much of it. But the typical dog probably has less hair in its armpits than the typical coed, if the coed is a Nirvana fan. And that tail thing could probably be put to some interesting uses during . . .

I admit the dog idea of cuisine is disgusting. But many's the human bride who ought to have buried her dinner in the yard. Dogs smell, but so do we men. And, one more thing—the kids are going to be ugly. But when we're out in that muddy duck blind, telling our son the solemn truths about how it is between men and women, we will, if we marry a dog, be able to give the boy one truly important word of instruction: "Fetch!"

P. J. O'Rourke

INTRODUCTION

This book contains all that is known in the world about women. Nothing has been omitted. Next time somebody collars you with one of those woman-trouble questions, pick up this little volume, turn to the handy index, and read to them out loud.

This is a book for men. It is not a book for women, even though women are transfixed by what men say about them. Women are certainly a big part of men's lives—usually more important than cars, careers, political science, or sports. So maybe this is a special interest reference book, like one of those Chilton guides to Hondas. For normal men who find life with normal women sometimes perplexing, this book might be just the ticket, since it was lab-tested under harsh clinical conditions, what with consulting lots of other men and asking them lots of personal questions.

But don't take it all too seriously, and don't sit down and try to read it cover to cover. Only money (or heartache) will cause a fellow to discuss women at such extraordinary length. And besides, listening to men talk about women for a long time is wearying, unproductive, and unnatural. Look what it did to Clarence Thomas and Joe Biden.

CHAPTER ONE

MODERN LOVE

FALL IN

Here's the scene: A normal guy gets up, puts on his suit, and leaves for work. He's a brown-shoe guy, normal in every way, regular as a traffic light. Up ahead is the office. He picks lint off his tie, glances up at his beautiful secretary standing in the office window, and starts across the street.

But the cover is off the manhole. Everyone can see it. People stop to watch the disaster. It's like a cheat-sheet for a Greek tragedy, where everyone except the hero knows something's wrong. Sure enough, his chin still up, the guy hits the hole mid-stride and it seems that in a nanosecond he's going to be up to his neck in trouble.

That's One Way. Here's the scene in replay. The guy looks at his beautiful secretary, starts across the street, the cover's off the manhole, the guy falls. But in a flash, he's popping his head up through the manhole opening, fresh as a daisy. Hey, you say, how did he do that? Well, it's a gimmick shot in a movie of the mundane, and the hero is just a normal stuntman, a guy with a great talent for falling and never, ever getting hurt.

Alas, the ability to take a fall over and over without showing scars and bruises is a learned skill, one we generally miss because at the time we need that sort of knowledge most, we're living in the suburbs of stupidity, head over heels for some dame.

A True Story, but a Parable Nonetheless. Once a certain Modern Man found himself unloading a cargo of U.S. AID groceries off a decrepit freighter airplane for the Cuban army at an Angolan Communist government outpost surrounded by rebel zealots supported by the CIA. It seems unlikely, but it happened, and more than once. One day there was an Englishman there, one of the flight crew, and he stood around for a while chatting in the shade of a wing while Uncle Sam fed the mad dogs of Marxism. The modern fellow gestured toward the Cuban soldiers and mentioned that he was nervous.

"Do you mean that you're frightened?" the Englishman asked.

You bet. So they talked about fear and anxiety for a while until he asked the Brit—a chap who'd been in maybe a half-dozen civil wars like the one in Angola—what sort of close call had frightened him most.

Not blind-drunk Ugandan fanatics, not midair engine failures, none of that. That wasn't it at all. "When I met my wife," he said. He'd always thought he was a cheerful bachelor, but when the affair changed from dating to destiny, he left the planet for a while. "I was so nervous that I shot myself in the foot."

How come?

"I don't know. I guess I'd heard about men doing that to keep them out of the army. It seemed like the right sort of thing to do."

No Deferments. By the time of this little chat, he'd been married twelve years. Still walked with a limp.

WHEN YOU GO NUTS

The point of all this is to suggest the essential irrationality of some situations—specifically, situations in which you have no control over what happens to you in the end. Smart guys avoid these situations. Oh, we fool around, of course. By and large, though, our common sense tells us to stay away from window ledges, open airplane doors, tall trees in a storm. But not women.

That's why we call it *"falling* in love."

WHAT TO KEEP WHEN YOU LOSE YOUR HEAD

As we noted in *The Modern Man's Guide to Life,* courtship is where life most resembles death, where love meets war, and thus where anything goes. Sometimes love seems like something cracked up by the Chilean secret police; when you fall in love with a woman, you are volunteering to submit yourself to the emotional equivalent of a government experiment in pain, torture, and disorientation.

Hide Your Valuables. No matter what happens, make sure you put the following items in a safe place, so that when the storm subsides, you'll still have a life:

- Your friends,
- your job,
- your bank account, and
- your favorite hangout.

If your romantic adventure doesn't work out, you'll mistakenly think that you have misplaced your self-esteem and your dignity. In fact, you'll find both right where you left them before the whole mess started. But forget about your common sense; you'll lose that first, and you won't get it back until much, much later.

LOOKING FOR TROUBLE

Love lurks in alleys and around blind corners, so as a rule you can be reasonably sure you'll never meet an interesting woman in any of the predictable places. In fact, if you picked up this little book hoping it would give you just that sort of insight, you missed a good shot. Take this book back where you bought it. The place where you meet women in a bookstore is clearly and appropriately marked SELF-HELP. Wait there. Something'll happen.

Here's where not to go:

THE TEN WORST PLACES TO MEET WOMEN

1. *Bars and Taverns.* The women you meet at bars will have their availability well-upholstered with desperation. Only museums and supermarket frozen food sections will offer such a wide range of truly lonely people. If you're a lonely guy yourself, then you already know that loneliness leaves you vulnerable; it's like a crippling ailment, of which you hope somebody will quickly take advantage.

2. *Personal Ads.* Sure, sure, everybody thinks of answering a personal ad sometime. It's an attractive proposition because you figure anyone who has to humiliate herself to the extent of advertising her availability couldn't possibly reject *you*. Wrong. The personal ads are for people who never learned how to say "Hello" with conviction. When you descend into the love-wanted ads, you're entering a world populated by the chronically cruel, the congenitally untouchable, the scabrous, and the ugly, all of whom hope to find mates in order to perpetuate their anomalous variety of humanity.

So if nothing else is working for you, give it a shot. Just, for God's sake, don't tell anybody about it later. One otherwise perfectly normal man became obsessed with the personals column in *The New York Review of Books.* Not to be cruel, but think about that for a sec: Lonely *New York Review of Books* readers looking for romance. Why don't they advertise in something racy—say, maybe, *New Republic?* Anyway, the guy ended up on a date with what must be a typical *New York Review of Books* want-ad woman—an intense, urgent psychologist of grim visage. But here's the little twist: At the same time the guy was regularly dating *Morgan Fairchild.* What was he thinking?

3. *Work.* We're told over and over not to mess around with coworkers, and for good reason. When the romance is over, so is the job for one or the other of you: You absolutely cannot function well in a job where one of your colleagues is a former mattress mate. And even if the two of you succeed in ignoring the situation, nobody else will: After all, most workplaces mass-produce boredom as a nondisposable by-product, and for everyone in the office, a failed affair will have the same compelling quality as a school bus plunge or a prostitution bust. Don't defer the decision on this one: Make up your mind whether or not you think your prospective lover is worth your job.

Beyond all those considerations, remember that using seduction as a means of getting ahead is a unisex gambit, and many of the women you meet at work will come armed with a scabbard containing a double-edged sword: An ambitious woman at work sees romance as a weapon.

On the other hand, where else is a busy chap going to meet somebody with whom he will already have much in common? So, if you're determined to follow a bad hunch, here are some hot tips to remember:

- *At all costs avoid* relationships with women who are your immediate subordinates or over whom you exert any potential professional influence. The road to sexual harassment hell is smoothly paved with such ill-formed intentions.
- *Get out:* If you work for a large company and the romance gets serious, one of you should transfer to another division of the company or organization. If you work for a smaller business, one of you should look for another job.
- *She's on top:* The most sensible relationship will be one with a woman who is your superior at work. The costs of high-risk romance are much easier for you to calculate if you're the one who's going to pay.
- *Get it down:* If you're going to get involved with the woman in the next cubicle, wait until the third date (see below) and discuss the inevitable complications; make sure she understands the consequences of the affair before you run the risk of screwing up your job.

This subject is also treated quite exhaustively in Chapter Three, "Modern Women at Work."

4. *School.* By schoolgirls, here, what we mean is your basic much-younger woman. Women's bones keep growing until they turn thirty, and one of those bones is the noggin. Hence, women often don't turn into grown-ups until sometime in their late-twenties, if then. (Men, with no such scientific excuses, defer such postadolescent transformations until they reach their mid- or late-thirties.) So, if she is still of tender age—or if you are, for that matter—the person with whom you're now involved will one day soon just be somebody with whom you *used* to be involved before all those changes took place.

5. *Hair Salons.* Hair salons are odd places, little frontier outposts of fashion filled with gender confusion, talking mousseheads, and hapless souls caught with their wet hair down. Besides, Modern Men patronize barbershops on principle, since they're virtually the only all-male environment left in America, the *real* hair clubs for men. Once women find out that men like to hang out in barbershops and talk about baseball and fishing, things could turn ugly: Imagine "Today" 's Katie Couric with a crew cut or NPR's Nina Totenberg with a flattop and fenders.

6. *Gym.* It's not that women in gyms are undesirable. In fact, by virtue of being there at all, they manifest a certain kind of attractiveness—especially since you know what you're getting into, physique-wise. The trouble is, so do they. No matter how great you look later, she'll always remember the way you looked the first time she saw you—fat, sweaty, blowing air like a choo-choo.

7. *Vacation.* It's never the same once you get back to Earth.

8. *The ABA, AMA, ADA, or Any Other National Convention.* Shared interests are fine. But so is a shared geography, and the trouble with pitching woo at somebody you meet from Denver when you live in Portland is that after a while your arm gets tired and your game goes to hell and you've got to face her again the very next year.

9. *Clinics*—rehab, eating disorder, whatever. Outpatient relationships are always a little less encumbered than courtships carried out in encounter groups.

10. *The Worst Place to Meet a Woman Is in a Court of Law,* what with her lawyers and your lawyers and all. If you would avoid number ten on our little list, read again one through nine.

That's the view from the bottom of the barrel.

A FOOLPROOF WAY TO PICK UP WOMEN

Face the subject. Bend your legs slightly. Grasp her firmly in your arms just above her knees. Lift, using your legs—not your back—to do the work. Allow her waist to bend over your shoulder. Keep your weight forward.

That's the only way to do it. Try anything else, and you'll be flat on your back, metaphorically, since women are never more ruthless than when deflecting an awkward pick-up attempt. Besides, while women tend not to take guys on the make very seriously, they do respond rather well to politeness and humor, interesting conversation, and a subordination of testosteronal mindwarps.

So, when you're ready, here's a rundown of

THE TEN BEST PLACES TO MEET A WOMAN

1. *On Line.* While it's the least desirable of all the desirable places to meet a woman, you're okay anyplace a queue has formed because of bureaucratic or corporate inefficiency—the motor vehicles department or the bank, for example, or anyplace else where a common enemy has conspired to toss the two of you together on the stormy sea of institutional incompetence.

2. *Fires.* There's nothing like sharing the experience of watching your apartment building go up in flames to bring two neighbors a little closer together.

3. *Hospitals* are filled with women paid to care. The trick is to get them to stop seeing you as a patient—without a loss in the quality of their attention.

4. *Restaurants.* Waitresses are made to be wed. There is something absolutely compelling about a good-looking woman coming at you with plenty of good food in both hands.

5. *Weddings,* except watch out for topical conversation.

6. *AA Meetings.* Two different people from two different states and from two different genders said this. But isn't there a rule about this sort of thing?

7. *On Airplanes*—but only if you're lucky. What appears to be wife-for-life material on takeoff can easily turn into extra baggage on arrival.

8. *Churches or Clubs.* Churches, synagogues, and professional organizations are swell places to meet women. Like the people you meet at work, women you meet at clubs or in churches come with a ready supply of shared interests. But unlike the women you meet at work, the only material thing you stand to lose if love falters is your dues-paying status.

9. *Parties.* Parties are great, the second-best place to meet a woman. And the best of all parties is somebody else's office party.

10. *The Best Place to Meet a Woman Is at the End of the Aisle.* She'll never look better, and neither will you.

THE RULE OF DOUBLE EYE CONTACT ON A SINGLE OGLE

Everybody Ogles. We ogle, you ogle, he and she ogles, they ogle. Normally, of course, an ogle is like a tree falling unheard in a forest; an uncaught ogle only has meaning for the ogler. But what does it mean when a woman catches you ogling her and in return gives you a direct stare, not once, but *twice?*

The elements of this case are simple: Two adjacent-to-middle-aged guys. A mall. An escalator. One woman, mid-thirties. One ogle. Two eye contacts.

The details: A sunny day, but brisk. Two friends—we'll call them

Hoot and Gib—decide to meet for lunch at a downtown enclosed shopping mall. There's a quick dash into a Brooks Brothers outlet, where a suit is purchased within three minutes. Then there's lunch.

The dining area at the mall is one of those American adaptations of a Euro-trough, the standard street café, where people sit and look at other people until they are caught, at which time they stare intently at their corned beef sandwiches. Next to the café is an escalator, and next to the descending half of the escalator is where our two chaps encamp for a quick bite. One guy, Gib, is married, and he has his back to the escalator. In terms of passing women, he's in a blind spot: He can't see anything, and that's just as well. The other guy, Hoot, is single, and he can see everything. The escalator practically dumps shoppers at his feet.

The conversation is a heavily fragmented one. Gib, the married man, his back to the scenery, is talking about media coverage of the deficit. Hoot is frequently distracted by the sudden appearance and descent of one or another metropolitan beauty. In the middle of a sentence, typically, Hoot clams up, raises one eyebrow in a sullen smolder, and, frankly, ogles. He's been doing this for years, of course, so his scan is a well-practiced one. As a face man, he starts there. The face is his screening device. Bad face, back to the deficit. Good face, go directly to the shoes and work back up to the face. He ogles like a bibliophile, like a man who knows *exactly* which details and nuances create desirability, and which ones are fatal flaws. Gib waits patiently for the appraisal.

The Ian Brown Corollary. Men ogle not only to fantasize about women, but also to see how they themselves measure up as men.

The mall ogler's pastime is not a gender-specific one, of course. Women ogle as much as the next guy. Usually, they ogle other women, although since their mission in ogling is essentially fact-gathering—why did she wear *that* scarf? you call that green mold *eye shadow?* nice pumps—it may be demeaning to ogling to call it ogling. Women sometimes ogle men. That's ogling. Ogling is when you look at somebody in an effort not so much to evaluate the person being ogled as to evaluate your own ogling self.

Generally—and there are certainly exceptions to this corollary—an ogler is making a precise calculation that involves this equation: Self-image divided by her beauty plus her availability equals relative worth of ogler. There are many tiny variables that can nudge the ultimate solution one way or another. For instance, you might look at a beautiful passerby and find she is almost certainly out of the range of your ability to attract women. Maybe the self-image part of the equation is just too low, or her beauty + availability number is just too high. But then you say to yourself, "Sure, that's now. But with a dash of Rogaine, a few years on Somali-Fast, and a Samsonite full of C-notes, she'd be at my feet." Suddenly, your projected self-image numbers rise, and you find it more and more likely that not only could she be yours (if you really wanted) but that maybe you wouldn't have time for her, what with all the other women around.

But back to the Double Eye Contact on a Single Ogle Rule: Sometimes in ogling, as in all relationships, things sort of sneak up on you. For instance, after a burger-and-fries'-worth of idle ogling, Hoot suddenly pales. "I got eye contact," he says tensely, almost grimly. "No, wait. That's *it*." His voice drops to a heavy whisper. "I got *double eye contact*."

The sequence is this:

- Contact.
- Ignition.
- Lift-off.

So Hoot had cause to pause. Double eye contact in response to a single, lingering ogle is a gesture of commitment more meaningful than many marriages. When a woman returns an ogle with a mere single glance, it can mean anything. Might mean: What's-he-staring-at-is-there-toilet-paper-on-my-shoe? Might mean: Let's-see-what-kind-of-jerk-I'm-dredging-off-the-bottom-of-the-gene-pool-today. Might mean: Make-a-move-and-I-call-the-cops. Hence, most men disregard the single-glance-to-an-ogle response. Single glances used to mean something.

But with the widespread availability of go-go dancers, all of whom are quite accomplished in the art of making prolonged single-gesture eye contacts with oglers in bulk, a glance doesn't carry much weight anymore.

A double glance in response to an ogle, however, is something else. Double eye contact on a single ogle means this: I know you're watching me and I think you're sort of marginally interesting and I think I'll see what you're made of, buster.

So. You ogle. She does a double take. Now what do you do? If you look away, too stunned or embarrassed to continue ogling, you're scrapple. A guy too cowardly to stand up for his own ogle isn't much of a man in most women's books. But if you continue to ogle in the face of a double glance, the ball's back in her court. If she looks away, no point. If she smiles, you can figure you've been asked to politely identify yourself, your motives, your marital standing. If your papers are in order, you get permission to cross the line, to go the next step. Whatever that is.

The Never-Fail Principle of Bad Timing. Women almost never return an ogle until your wife or girlfriend is looking—first at the woman, wondering who she's smiling at, then at you, when she figures it out.

Because men ogle as a means of taking stock of themselves, they know there's nothing intrinsically threatening to the whole activity. Men don't ogle, after all, because they *want* to. They ogle because they *have* to. It's horrible. Call it *ogle burden*. It's what we do, and sometimes a man's gotta do what a man's gotta do.

That's why different men ogle in different ways. Involved men out with the objects of their involvement do an indirect ogle. They look around the supermarket as if they'd never seen anything quite like it before. Look at those lighting fixtures! they seem to be saying. And how about those metal shelving units! Their necks are suddenly rubberized for such occasions, and the fact that a clearly ogleable woman just happens to be in line of sight is pure coincidence. That way, if the woman oglee responds to the ogle with a smile, the guy can always look at his ferocious wife and shrug. Men know they can ogle their brains out and never get so much as a notice until one fine, spring day when an ogling kind of guy and his principal sugar-pie are out for a stroll. He tosses off an inconsequential ogle and presto! he gets a double- . . . no! a *triple*-take in return. Then he starts explaining.

Guys out in packs do competitive ogling. A woman walks down the street and there's a pack of wild oglers staring at her. She nervously glances over to make sure they aren't armed oglers, and instantly every man jack claims eye contact. "She was *looking* at me, man," one of them says, while the others produce documentary evidence refuting the claim.

Of all ogles, though, a single-man ogle is a serious thing. Women know that. That's why they never seem to respond with the rare double eye contact.

The Law of the Knowing Glance. The glance-to-ogle scenario has many variations. One of them involves the situation reversed, where she is the ogler and you are the objectified human, the oglee. There are two basic ways of handling this. One involves ignoring the ogle, a decision made after the all-important first glance. She ogles. You glance. In a split second, you have to process a great deal of information, all of it effervescently superficial and exactly the kind of information on which men make all important decisions, like whether or not to look again.

If you take the second look, you might be well-advised to invoke the Law of the Knowing Glance, which says an ogle is always trumped by a leer. In other words, you *slowly* look up and meet her gaze, while on your face you wear an expression that says, Was that good for you?

This has the effect of ram-injecting the encounter and giving it a NASA-level rate of acceleration. Suddenly, you're not just two strangers exchanging goggles for gapes. You're not only on intimate terms, but you're also in the driver's seat because you saw her ogle and raised her an innuendo. You can't lose. If she looks away, give her five minutes, and she'll ogle again. If she smiles, you can figure your glance was good enough that you can roll over and go to sleep. Either way, you'll have this encounter in the bag, if you'll pardon the play on words.

The Obviated Ogle Injunction. An ogle is diminished by overshadowing eccentricities. Let's say you're sitting alone in a subway car when a gaggle of art school painters' models—women who have been ogled with aesthetic passion—gets in. They're young, they're beautiful, and they stare right at you. The significance of their attention will depend on why they're staring. If you're wearing a Santa suit and darning your socks, all ogles are off. No return glances are scored, and your self-image numbers are expressed in negatives.

MOJO

Mojo ought to be on the periodic table of elements or on the government's list of restricted substances.

Symptoms. Dangerous stuff, as you know if you've seen it at work. You're walking down the street and suddenly you realize that every woman you pass is making eye contact with you. You go into a restaurant, and the waitress asks your name. On transcontinental flights, the cabin attendant moves your seat so she can sit next to you. When you have mojo, no woman is safe. Mojo caps your teeth, reforests your head, trims your waist, and clips your nose hairs. Mojo is a secret musk, a vibe the size of Lionel Hampton's.

Mass Mojo. Mojo circulates inside a group of friends in a curious fashion. Let's say you wake up one morning with mojo. All morning long, women are smiling at you, giving you the once-over, treating you as if you were employed full-time. Then you meet your pals for lunch. The waitress forgets to take your order. Why? Because she's busy telling one of your chums about her vacation in Greece and wondering out loud why there's no stiletto-heel rental concessions on all those Mediterranean nude beaches. Until the moment you walked into the diner, you had mojo. Your buddy had no mojo. But something happened—your pal will call it a miracle, you'll call it a catastrophe—because now, *for no* *good reason,* your buddy has mojo, and you don't. You got no mo' mojo. You may not get your mojo back for *years.*

So think of mojo the same way you would low interest rates: When you get mojo, completely refinance your love life, collect all that mojo equity, and, if you're feeling flush, see Chapter Four, "Modern Cohabitation."

LUST-IDENTIFICATION FOR CIVILIANS

Two guys walking down the street. The Municipal Beauty-on-Duty passes within, say, two feet of their very persons. One guy says to the other guy, "I love her." Other guy nods.

No. Wrong. Not love. Lust. It's important to distinguish love from infatuation and infatuation from lust, and to confuse none of these with obsession.

Lust. We assume you know the difference between infatuation and lust, just as you presumably know the difference between your genitals and your heart. If, for example, you look into her eyes when you talk to her, it's probably infatuation. If, on the other hand, you look down her blouse when you talk to her, it may well be lust. It's *definitely* lust if you push her head back and out of the way to get a better look down her blouse when you talk to her.

Where serious infatuation is usually the first step to long-term romance, lust is occasionally the first step to infatuation (see below). If that happens, you can figure lust to have a life span of three months or so. After that, it's trouble. Nothing's uglier than lust beached and floundering on the shores of reality.

So remember, it goes like this: Lust, infatuation, *then* love. What women call love at first sight is really lucky lust.

Lost in Lust. Trouble is, lust looks *exactly* like love; even an expert can't tell them apart, so be careful here. If you find yourself being pulled loins-first into a liaison you think might be ill-advised, excuse yourself, go to the men's room, and look at yourself in the mirror while you slowly count to fifty. When you return to the source of the heat, try to imagine what she'd look like with chow in the spaces between her teeth. Do *anything* you can to put the brakes on. Even the most savvy guy sometimes wakes up too late and wonders how his brains wound up in his briefs.

The Difference Between Infatuation and Obsession Is Critical. It's *obsession* if you know in your heart you don't have a ghost of a chance, but you can't stop chasing her because you somehow think you *ought* to chase her. Obsession is your problem; it has absolutely nothing to do with the person you're pursuing and almost everything to do with all the other garbage in your life.

It's *infatuation* if you know with some degree of certainty that she shares your romantic ambition.

In other words, the difference between obsession and infatuation is that if you're simply obsessed, you'll never woo and win her, no matter what; if you're infatuated, you may have already won her affection, even if you don't know it.

Choose Your Poison. Infatuation is available in a million makes and models, from sporty little runabouts to heavy-duty family wagons, each with a specific virtue and a nonnegotiable price, and each designed to transport you someplace you may think no man has ever gone before.

But infatuation is a kind of twilight zone, and in spite of all our warnings, *when you become infatuated with a woman, you have ceased to live among men with operating and delimiting senses.* You have moved into a strange state of suspended rationality. You're trapped in a soundproof booth made of one-way glass. A smart fellow will go into that nether region equipped with notes tucked up his sleeve. And one of those little bits of paper should have written upon it "The First Law of Infatuation": By the time you realize you're infatuated with a woman, you're already in love with her.

AVAILABILITY

Respect a Woman's Private Life. If she's wearing a wedding ring, don't try to fast-talk it off her finger—you'll just look like a jerk to her and to anyone else who might be watching.

Some women, however, are on the confused cusp of availability, and a little conversational exploration is necessary. But don't get involved in some overproduced detective movie: If it seems probable that a dinner invitation wouldn't be a social gaffe, then tender one. If you aren't sure, try for lunch. Lunch is a natural prequel to a real date, sort of like living together through dessert. If she says something that sounds like she's involved in an entangling alliance, just smile politely and drop the whole thing. See if she picks it up.

WOMEN WHO ARE AVAILABLE IN THEORY, BUT NOT TO YOU

Here's a short list of women who might be available, all right, but who will deliver a lot more trouble than you bargained for:

- Your boss. How many times do I have to tell you?
- Your boss's ex-wife.
- Your lawyer's ex-wife.
- Your ex-wife's best friend.
- Your best friend's ex-wife.
- Your girlfriend's daughter, stepdaughter, adopted daughter, whatever.
- Your best friend's girlfriend, no matter what.

MEN AND MANNERS

Let's stop here for a second, brush off those lapels, straighten that tie, and see how you're looking. Every now and then, a guy ought to send himself out to be pressed, just to remind himself what he looked like before he wrestled with romance and trashed the deportment department. Often it seems when we lose our head, we lose our civility.

Henry Morton Stanley, the famous explorer, was one of the rudest men of his time. As a discoverer of African landmarks, he was a fraud and a cheat. As a leader of men, he was a tyrant and a murderer. As a European in Africa, he was a native-hating thug, shooting and killing his way through the bush. But Stanley was blessed with the modern gift of media manipulation, and he knew that what marked a true Victorian hero more than anything else was civility under pressure. That's why, after a much-publicized "search" for David Livingstone, a gently inquisitive missionary never lost, Stanley—and we have only his word for this—greeted the object of his self-serving stunt with a cheerful, "Dr. Livingstone, I presume?" That single, somewhat deferential and dissembling "I presume" catapulted Stanley into history, of course, and when his movie was made, Spencer Tracy played the part, and not Edward G. Robinson.

If you're not well-behaved now, there's nothing that's going to make you shape up at this point in your life—unless there's something in it for you, right? So let's be practical; let's learn from our man Stanley: The thing about good manners is they can mask a truly odious character: You can run into a stranger's house, piss in all the corners, puke on the frozen burritos, light your farts, and ridicule the baby, and, provided you do these things with grace and aplomb, you'll be invited back when you can stay a little longer, for good manners are the little pink air freshener in the butt-filled urinal of life, the shiny tuxedo that cloaks the thickly stained skivvies of existence, the Kitty Litter in the cat box of modern mayhem, if you get the idea.

Ladieees and Gennelmen

Of course, the mess surrounding modern manners has not been made by man alone. One very good reason there are so precious few gentlemen wandering the planet is that there's a real shortfall in the global supply of ladies. Until the hideous children of the postwar baby boom showed up with their full complement of progress and rectitude, the job of maintaining the liturgy of civilization was left to women. Women governed our homes and taught our children.

No more. So let's just assume that manners are a man's job: Men must do the polite thing because it's the right thing. After all, it's the business of Modern Men to bear the burden of keeping well-oiled the machinery of society and to recivilize the world—starting, of course, with rude women.

But remember, only men can be gallant. Treat women to old-fashioned courtesies—*but only if you can do so without being rudely ostentatious.* Stand when a woman approaches you. Tip your hat, if you wear one. Hold that door, light that cigarette, steady that chair—all without calling undue attention to yourself, and regardless of what others may say.

Courtliness and gallantry are gentlemanly traits, and manly manners just aren't women's work. So men must follow the rules of conduct without attaching any significance whatsoever to any reaction women may have to good behavior—although it should be pointed out that good manners have a certain aphrodisiac effect on most women—and without paying any heed to changing social fashions and fads.

THE MAIN MANNERS

When you strip away all the etiquette-book specificity and all the complicated dinner-table fork-swapping, there are only five basic rules of manly behavior:

1. *Don't make animal noises at women.* For some reason, women find men who bark like a horny beagle somewhat obnoxious, and, strange as it may seem to some men, women actually don't get turned on by men who do kennel impersonations. Not only that, but hormone-benumbed men yelling "Arf!" at women in the middle of the street humiliate other, less feral guys.

2. *Don't whine or complain.* The recent vogue that has men weeping over each other's misfortune is, in many ways, only a weak justification for violating a key tenet of manly manners: stoicism. This is not to say that men must not bleed when they are cut, but it is to say that if you are keen on overdeveloping your sensitivity, those around you would appreciate you rehearsing your suffering in private before taking the show on the road.

3. *Don't be a politician in your personal life.* A charitable man might be able to raise an argument in favor of falsehoods, especially those that serve a noble purpose. But, by and large, a lie hurts more than the truth, and a savvy chappy will substitute tact for invention whenever possible.

Some professions are based on lies, and self-serving ones at that. *All* politicians, for example, lie on a casual and routine basis, since much of what they do involves disguising their base ambitions and their manifold failures. If you don't believe it, just read his lips. Or sign his petition. Or watch him exhale without inhaling. Or let him give you a ride home from the party.

4. *Don't hit.* Look, you're probably an average Joe—maybe not to you, of course, or to your mom—but stat-wise, you probably fit right next to most of us there in the big number bulge, about halfway along the spectrum of humanity. That means that all of the people on Earth can pick on you some of the time, and half the people can pick on you all of the time.

But they don't, do they? All those wily Egyptians, inscrutable Chinese, and excitable Poles who could be yanking your chain but aren't should be a lesson to you. Be kind, be gentle. And don't, under any circumstances, ever, *ever* hit women or children.

The reciprocal here is simple kindness. Kindness is manners without forethought. For example, it's a kind thing when you surrender your train seat to a pregnant woman or a woman trying hard to control a toddler.

5. *Don't sell your family short.* Family comes before friendship; friendship comes before your job; your job comes last. Keep your best manners for those closest to home; it's rude to ask your wife or your family to take second place to something as intrinsically meaningless as a job. On the other hand, if you've already subordinated your family to your work to the point of destroying the former, it's also rude to avoid the responsibility of supporting your children.

The point of this extremely obvious list is that decent deportment starts from down deep, like a tune by Pavarotti. Good manners are based on common sense and implied values, and the rules of etiquette—the labyrinthine rituals of social behavior—are only manifestations of a belief in the sort of common-sense virtues listed here. Idi Amin, for example, may have known well the rules of etiquette, but, in the final analysis, he was extremely ill-mannered, something his citizens did not discover until after they had been invited for dinner.

Dating Etiquette. Examine your motives. There are, after all—and despite the message of *When Harry Met Sally* and other films—women who make pleasant date-type companions, and for whom you may feel no baser ambition than friendship. On the other hand, if the object of your courtship is to persuade a woman to get naked and tell you she loves you, then mind your p's and q's, since often the fastest way to a woman's lingerie is to politely ask her to remove her outer clothing.

• *Don't make sex the object of your date.* Nothing leaves a dirty stain on a first or second date like the sweaty ring of desperation.

• *Make the date decisions yourself.* Don't call a woman, ask her out, then ask her where you're going. Take charge. A date shouldn't be confused with democracy.

• *Talk to your date.* Try to avoid staring, glassy-eyed, at her chest;

listen to what she is saying, and ignore the heaving of her lungs while she's saying it.

· *Memorize the basic rules of woman-herding.* Help her into her coat; hold the car door for her; hold her chair when she sits; escort her into and out of the restaurant; stand if she leaves the table during dinner, and again when she returns; don't try to kiss her if it looks like wrestling might be involved; make sure she gets home safely. These are fundamental rules of etiquette. Perform them easily and gracefully. Don't be a stiff.

· *Call her again* if you enjoyed being with her. Don't escalate the who-calls-whom routine into a game. You'll lose.

HERE'S WHAT HAPPENS WHEN YOU ASK A WOMAN TO GO ON A DATE

When you invite a woman to spend an evening with you, every gesture, every word is an unmarked path and any one of them may lead you into a dark wood where all those things that were safe and familiar will turn into demons of the night, some of which may be real. Once, back in the sixties, people had experience distinguishing fantasy from reality: The snakes on the wall were just the drug talking. These are straighter times, friend. Those really are snakes.

DATE DESIGN

A good date is just like a TV movie, in that it has a beginning, a middle, and an end. Beyond that, each of the first three dates has a special significance and is a component of a unique sort of progression: If the first three dates go well, you're on the stairway to heaven. If they don't, you're in the subbasement and on the escalator down.

First Date. First dates are horrible social circumstances chock-full of mystery, tension, and insecurity, made by the same fine folks that bring you important job interviews and meetings with remarkable dentists.

With that in mind, here's the bottom line up top: Keep a first date simple. This isn't grand opera you're plotting here, pal. Just plan a pleasant and unpretentious evening. Remember that the purpose of a first date is to confirm an initial attraction—on both sides, presumably—and to get to know one another, so build in a little flexibility and keep the whole thing casual, at least psychologically. The cause of tension on a first date is control. A first date is a day trip into the unfamiliar, where both of you will be trying to control unpredictable circumstances. So keep things somewhat predictable.

In fact, don't do anything that adds to the inherent discomfort of a first meeting. What we're talking about is something like dinner, and, if you seem to be enjoying yourself, maybe some dancing, or a nightcap at a bar or nightclub. What we're *not* talking about is a crowded schedule full of stops at every cool, quaint, or chic spot you've ever heard of. One guy worked *seven* stops into a three-hour date. The woman later said she felt like she'd changed planes in Frankfurt and had taken the city tour during the layover. A first date isn't a platform for you to try to impress yourself or your date, and it isn't an episode of "This Is My Life." Above all, a first date isn't a contest with sex as a prize.

Here are some other things to keep in mind:

• *Plan ahead.* If you ask somebody out, you ought to know with a dead certainty where you'd like to go. But don't orchestrate the evening so tightly that you preclude any spontaneity, since she may have a good idea of her own. Be willing to scrap your plans at the drop of a reasonable alternative.

• *Comfort counts.* Pick a place with which you are familiar and where you will feel somewhat in control. The best way to impress a first date is to be genuinely at ease. After all, one of the ultimate goals of a good romance is a balance of mutually assured comfort.

• *Separate yourselves from the crowd.* Choose a restaurant that offers both the chance for conversation and the opportunity to do a little people-watching. Save the more intimate venues for a second or third date.

• *Sure, sure,* you're *interesting—but so is your date.* Ask her a question and listen to her answer. Remark on her answer, then ask more questions. This is called conversation and it's powerfully seductive. Any woman who matters will always respond to a man who is genuinely interested in her interests. If you make a woman feel *interesting,* you've also made her feel somehow more attractive. And you've gone a long way toward making her think that *you're* interesting and attractive.

• *Don't seek reassurance.* Not on a first date, not on a third date, not ever. Women can sniff out fear and insecurity. Keep yours well-hidden for life.

• *Avoid future shock.* Don't discuss your hopes and dreams for a family and a picket-fence future. Don't talk about favorite baby names. If you feel you *must* talk about the future, ask her how she feels about the new tax regulations as they apply to IRAs and other independent pension plans.

• *Don't ask her out* for a second date before the first date is over (see below).

• *Don't make a pass on a first date.* Remember, a date is not a contest. A simple kiss—or even a handshake—will suffice for a first date. If she expects anything more, you'll be the first to know.

• *Say good night, Gracie.* When you ask a woman to join you on a date, you're not volunteering for target practice. If your date is rude or gets uncontrollably drunk or starts giving you the all-women-are-victims-and-you're-an-oppressor lecture, take her home pronto. Don't lose your temper and don't abandon a date, no matter how obnoxious she becomes. Unless she specifically refuses to accompany you, you are obliged to return her where you found her.

First-Date Analysis. By the end of the first date, you will have a well-developed impression, not of the woman your date *actually* is, but of what you fervently *hope* she might be. Try your best to separate the two, since any confusion you bring forward from this point on will only haunt you later.

Think it over before you ask her out again. If you had a nice time, your big question is going to be something dealing with reproductive magic. Men invariably measure romantic success by the tiny little yardstick they tote in their pants. So you'll want to know whether or not you can take her to bed, and the answer is always maybe, unless it's no.

Instead of asking yourself unanswerable questions, like whether or not she liked you, ask yourself some questions to which you have answers: Was she smarter than her salad? How would you feel if she showed up unexpectedly at your front door?

You get the idea.

One last first-date tip: The chances are, she'll never look better to you than she does on the first date.

Second Date. Round two is a confirming circumstance, in which your fantasy characterization will be seen to either hold water or not. Consequently, second dates should be casual and somewhat briefer than first dates. If during the first date she even comes close to meeting the expectations you projected, you'll find yourself in a state of militant euphoria after you drop her off. Cool off. Try to bring the same analytical method to the second date that you brought to the first one.

And one other thing about second dates: The second date is as important to her as it is to you. After all, she's not sitting there with you because there's nothing good on TV. Now is your chance to use all that body-lingo garbage you've been reading in women's magazines. Watch for dilated pupils, excessive laughter at your lamest one-liners, presenting behavior—lots of breast-thrusting, preening, and leaning into your conversation—and touching. Especially watch for touching. It's the dead giveaway, right? Let's say she's beauteous and let's say she has something to say about the tuna, and she leans forward and touches your sleeve as she says it, and your mind leaves your body for a mini-moment and melds with her mind and in a flash you see her hand on your sleeve *and* her head on your pillow all at once. Quite incredible, really.

Men don't touch a lot when we want to make a point, conversationally, so we really don't know what that touch means. But it's good. We know that. Lots of touching is really good. Lots of touching has us thinking grope, and grope is okay, too.

Second-Date Tactile Analysis. Let's step back a little and look at this through the eyes of a scientist. To determine touch-meaning and whether or not your attraction to your date is reciprocated, use the following chart to calculate the relationship between touches per hour of normal conversation in a public or semipublic place with the probability of substantive infatuative influences.

Third Date. If your third date goes well, you're a goner. On the basis of knowing a woman for only a few hours, you'll have made a significant emotional investment. You will have given someone you barely know an enormous amount of power over the happiness in your life. Consequently, a good third date can last for months, years even.

Conversely, it can also plant the seeds of the romance's destruction. How much objectivity can you muster? After all, those powerful assumptions you made about her on the first, second, and third dates might all be wrong, something you'll not find out until much, much later.

ROAD DATES AND AWAY GAMES

Going out to dinner with a stranger is one thing; going out of state with one is something else altogether. Many men are never happy with the full serving of difficulties dating hands them. They have to make it *more* difficult by taking their show on the road, somehow assuming that if women like them where they live, they'll *love* them where they don't, or something to that effect. There's nothing quite like jamming two almost-strangers together for a pressure-cooked spin out of control to turn love into hate. But don't listen to us. If you're one of those traveling sort of chaps, here's what you need to know about transporting a woman.

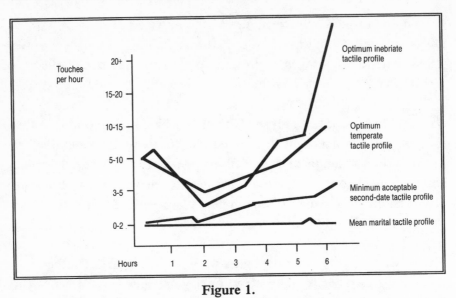

Figure 1.

The second-hour drop is characteristic of feminine hesitancy; provided responses are not forced, tactile phenomena should increase in frequency during the third, fourth, and fifth hours. By the sixth hour, you will have gleaned some important information. First, you can figure that if she's still with you after six hours, she either likes you or she's asleep. Second, if liquor is involved, by the sixth hour, she's either leaning all over you (driving the profile graph off the chart) or she's under the table.

Cheers. Life, to paraphrase Chaucer, is naught but a thoroughfare of woe. The world outside your car window is a nasty and toxic place, and the reflection you see in the glass is the face of a man who will one day be dead. Just kidding! Well, nothing like a little feminine company to sort of brighten the view. A beautiful woman, after all, is a kind of portable tourist attraction, where every roadside rest is a scenic overlook.

Ultimately, however, there are only three reasons to travel with women:

1. For romance.
2. For business.
3. To carry in the groceries.

Here, we're sticking with reason number one. Two and three are discussed elsewhere.

THE ESSENTIAL COMPANION

The passing planet outside your car, train, or plane will never be as compelling as the person sitting next to you—if the person sitting next to you is the person who *should* be sitting next to you. When it comes to travel, people in love—as well as those who find they aren't—quickly realize that where they go isn't nearly as important as the person with whom they are going. Not only that, but one overriding reason for traveling with the woman you love is that, given a choice, it would not only be unthinkable to leave her behind, it would also be bad for your romance. You would miss her, she would miss you, there'd be a missed phone call, a crossed signal, followed by undefined anxiety and a weird sort of long-distance pout. (One man tells the story of the hotel operator who put through his wife's late-night call to the wrong room, one occupied by a woman with a similar-sounding last name. The wife nearly moved to her mother's in the middle of the night. Took a week of explanations.)

If your romance is a new one, it helps to remember that love isn't really blind, and fear always walks point in an emotional conflict. Distance can magnify all these kinds of threats. In fact, you can, for example, be reasonably sure that if absence makes the heart grow fonder, the heart probably isn't tried—or, worse, true.

PITFALLS AND POTHOLES

Hey! Watch where you're going!

The elements of a travel date are remarkably similar to a stationary one:

1. *Take charge* of a travel date, but don't make your companion feel powerless. Hence,

2. *Uncomplicate things.* Ever see one of those charts that lists life's most stressful situations? There's imminent death, followed by divorce and impalement and the like. Someplace in that parade of disappointments is traveling, an activity in which participants are placed in a state of suspended alienation, stripped of control, subject to the hideous abuses of chance.

3. *Two elements.* It follows, then, that a date that involves traveling is no day at the beach, even if it's just a day at the beach, so all your planning must be directed toward two elements: comfort and security.

4. *Plan the trip.* If taking a weekend flier in the countryside is your idea, don't go off half-cocked. Plan *everything.* Know where you will eat; study the route you'll take; figure traveling times. Above all, book a room. Who knows why motels fill up in February? Conventioneers roam the land, gobbling up whole Motel 6s without a burp. Arriving without a reservation can turn a quiet, peaceful interlude into a grim circus, where the only clown your partner will see is you.

5. *The outer limits.* If your idea for a quick getaway has to fit into a two-day window of opportunity, don't shoot for the moon. Four hours is the maximum drive-time for a one-nighter—if you can start Saturday morning and come back Sunday night. Figure for yourself: Up at nine, leave by eleven, stop for lunch, stop for antiques, stop for gas, stop for a glider ride, stop to take a picture of a giant fiberglass cow, arrive at six-thirty, seven. Have a drink, wash up, out to dinner. Perfect. Add a mere two hours to that tranquil scenario, and you have a grueling day, where you arrive tired and famished just as the only restaurant in town

is closing. Your companion, made irritable by famine, picks a fight with you, and you end up sitting on the floor drinking alone watching CNN on motel cable while she sleeps in the bed.

When you figure time for a highway date, double the travel time for any distance beyond 100 miles. Assuming four hours drive-time the first day, add no more than ninety minutes of travel time for each additional day away, to a maximum of seven and a half hours per day for a transcontinental trek—which, by the way, is a lousy date idea.

6. *Location, location, location.* Again, assuming it's a one-night, two-day holiday by car we're talking about here, there are only a limited number of places close enough to reach on a road date. The rule of the road, woman-wise, is this: *The means justify the ends.* Travel with an anticipation of adventure, drive slowly, and stop frequently. Ideally, your destination should be a firm rebuttal of Machiavelli's famous axiom, since it really doesn't matter where you end a perfect day, so long as it's in a comfortable, safe, and pleasant place.

7. *Know the road.* Do your own navigating.

8. *Quickly resolve* even the smallest disputes. They fester fast when the relationship's in motion.

9. *Pack right.* Nothing can kill the spontaneous sense of freedom that travel brings faster than having to lug around too much junk. But take what you need, and if your companion asks you for advice, underestimate—you can always buy something on the spot. As for romance, if she asks what to wear, tell her to follow the rule of etiquette: If you don't have something nice to wear, don't wear anything at all.

10. *Boys at the wheel.* Finally, at the bottom of the common-sense barrel, *don't drive your dick.* In the movie in your mind, you may look cool cutting in and out of traffic and racing down suburban streets. To her, though, you'll look like a potential casualty of adolescence.

ITINERARIES

Keep in mind that subjecting a near-first date to both the incredible, wonderful newness of you and the frightening newness of nowhere is a double date with trouble twins. In a bar, for example, you can ask a strange woman if she wants to go for Italian food in Rome, and she'll laugh and say, "Sure." But if you show up on her doorstep with a couple of Alitalia tickets, she'll run for cover.

The virtue of a traveling date is that it provides a near-perfect us vs. them scenario, where together you face the big, bad world. Unhappily, the world is plenty big and bad enough already, so start with something small, something more symbolic of a travel-date. For instance, instead of picking her up at eight for supper, pick her up at five-thirty and head for the hills—that is, if you know of a restaurant there. A pleasant drive devoid of special effects and stunt maneuvers on a warm summer evening is a great way to create an atmosphere conducive to chatting. Make her radio monitor; it'll not only give you something to talk about, it'll also help you make sure you're not squiring around a potential groupie for Ratt.

LOVE ALERT

Know the Early Warning Signals

The key to prevention, as they say, is early detection. In the empire of our dreams, love comes as an insidious midnight Hun in disguise, ready to sack, loot, and pillage. Guard the gates.

After every date or encounter with the object of your fascination, check for the seven danger signals:

1. *Elation.* You are ecstatic. To you, it's incredible that someone as wonderful, beautiful, witty, whatever, as she obviously is actually seems

to be attracted to someone like you. It's amazing, it's remarkable, and, really, to everyone else, it's boring.

2. *The Critique.* You replay the game tape. You can't believe the number of awkward, inappropriate, and outright stupid things you said. You stand in front of the mirror; you see your hair the way she must have seen it, and you look like an experimental vegetable, something in the tuber family. You look at your jerky necktie and your ridiculous trousers and your once-fashionable jacket. You wonder why strangers didn't stop you on the street and warn you that you looked hideous.

3. *Apprehension.* You thought everything went well. At least, that's the way it seemed to you. But let's say at one in the morning you become absolutely *certain,* beyond the shadow of a doubt, that she acted like she liked you less this time than she did last time. By one-fifteen, you're convinced you'll never see her again, unless it's in the company of another man, and with a slightly cruel smirk on her face. *She knows you.* It's all over. You're sure of it.

4. *The Copernican Dilemma.* Suddenly you realize that she is at the center of everything you do and say. If you bump into one of her acquaintances on the street, you worry how everything you say will be edited for later rebroadcast; the books you buy are the books you think she thinks you ought to be reading; even when you know there's not a chance in the world of running into her, you dress as though you just *might*; when you're with your pals, she's the constant topic of your lame conversation.

5. *The Uri Geller Syndrome.* You watch doors and *will* her to walk through them; you stare at your telephone and *demand* that it ring.

6. *The Neediest Case.* You require an inordinate amount of reassurance—especially from the one person from whom you should never seek it. You analyze everything she does in terms of what it *means,* no matter how meaningless it is.

7. *Litmus test.* You act like a girl. (See above, one through six.)

If your behavior fits any of the categories above, you're in deep. Swim to the edge and get a grip. Look at the way you're behaving, man. Not to repeat this *ad infinitum,* but try to remember that you're in a state of obnoxious irrationality. In your confusion, you think you must seem like a sweaty, creepy, insecure jerk. But to your friends and those who know you well, you look very much like a guy in a clown suit juggling hamsters.

THE HIDEOUS HOLIDAY DATE

The long-winded tale of misery that begins each January and ends each December—a year, technically—is a narrative laced with disappointment, irony, and bitterness. It's a meaningless story with no plot, in which slowly accumulated hours of mindless tedium are punctuated with a few urgently executed celebrations of hypocrisy, guilt, and greed. We call these evanescent moments "the holidays," by which we mean Hanukkah, Christmas, and New Year's Eve. Together they constitute our season to be jolly.

The real function of the holidays is evident: At no other time do we so carefully scrutinize our apparent need for family ties and a religious background. And at no other time is a dating man's mettle more likely to be tested.

Let's pose a yuletide situation here, in which you—our model Modern Man, and a bachelor for the purposes of this illustration—are the recipient of that most feared of all holiday invites: a trip home to meet the parents of a woman whom you have come to know in a festive, carnal kind of way.

• *Pack right, pack light:* Take a blazer and a pair of khaki trousers, in addition to whatever else you're taking along. No matter how informal she swears to you it's going to be, the at-ease uniform of the Modern Man is what you'll want in order to avoid screwing up all the holiday pictures you're likely to be a part of. To her family, nothing marks you for life as a boor more than showing up in your clean-the-attic worst.

• *Take a camera,* and take lots of pictures of your girl, her dear old dog, her carping siblings, her cadaverous great aunt, her troll doll collection. When you drop the film off, ask for a set of dupes. Give one copy to the girl, and, if you still harbor ardor for her after the holiday, give her the other set to send home to her mother. Under separate cover, send a thank-you note.

• *Stay sober.* Remember, if her family gets drunk in front of you, they will ever after be trying to ingratiate themselves to you to prove they're not the assholes they seemed to be. But if you get drunk in front of them, you'll never live it down.

• *Don't take any drugs,* even if they are offered to you by her parents.

• *Keep your mouth shut.* Don't repeat in the living room the salacious gossip you picked up in the kitchen. Nothing brings a disintegrating family together like perceived ridicule from an outsider. Don't take sides in family squabbles.

• *Try to look interested* while everyone is opening gifts. Don't nod out or pretend to read that copy of *The Revolution Within* they gave you as a token of their deep esteem.

• *Don't try to win her family's affection* by showering them with expensive gifts. Remember, these are people you've never met before. The gift to her family that is in the best possible taste is the light touch with which you offer praise and nonthreatening affection to their daughter.

• *Mark her manners well.* If she embarrasses you in front of her family, she'll trash you in front of anyone, including her next boyfriend.

All in the Family. If she's coming home with you, make her the absolute priority. Don't introduce her to your family, then disappear with your brothers for an all-day touch football game. Keep her with you until she dismisses you or until you know beyond a doubt that she feels comfortable with your relatives.

THE FIRST BREAKFAST DATE

Sexually transmitted diseases notwithstanding, it's still a mistake to confuse sex with love. You'll know the difference between screwing and making love when it happens. Until then, you're safer assuming that sex has only one intrinsic meaning for her—or for you—and it's all summed up in three little words: Could kill you. So strive for premarital celibacy. If you fall short, consider:

First Aid. You have to use a condom. You *have* to. Pretend that if you don't, your face will turn into your butt and your dick will fall off. Using a condom is a most manly deed. Slip on that rubber, chum, and you not only greatly reduce the chances of spreading AIDS and other STDs, you also lower the rhetorical volume of a critically important national debate: If we all used condoms all the time, abortion wouldn't be an issue.

Let's assume you're a responsible citizen on your first sheet-tumble. There's an off-chance that you may, at some point, wonder what it all means. Read on.

A Woman's Place. If you make your dirty debut at her place, you're still wearing the red badge of probation. You'll see the museum of her life, but only the exhibits she has selected for public viewing: Everything is there for a reason. If some other guy's raincoat is on a coat hook, she knows it and she knows what it means to you.

A Man's Place. On the other hand, if she comes to your place, she's exhibiting a meaningful measure of trust. If you stay at her place, you'll be expected to leave in the morning. If she stays at your place, she'll expect to stay forever.

In that short, tension-filled moment when she first sets eyes on your bedchamber, anything can happen. She might, for example, bolt and run screaming into the night.

• *Don't invite a woman into a messy bedroom.* If you like her enough to go to bed with her, then respect her enough to get your briefs off the lamp shade and the Bud empties out from under the mattress. Don't go overboard here, but a bedroom that looks like it sheltered a convention of drunk bachelors isn't as seductive as you might think.

• *Don't festoon your room* with souvenirs of past conquests or artifacts that suggest your proclivity for rubber-and-handcuffs fantasies. One notorious cocksman kept a bagful of mementos—his dates' panties, as it happens—in his bedroom. A friend visited the place and said it smelled like a roomful of old, dirty underwear. Some musk.

• *Don't talk about your other girlfriends,* and don't keep their photographs around, either. Don't compare the woman you're with to any other woman on the planet.

• *Make your seduction as slow as your passion will allow.*

• *Don't suggest in any way that she should go home after you've made love.* And, if you're at her place, don't jump up after your nanosecond of biological significance and race out into the night. If you just *can't* hang around, suggest something—a craving for Thai food, maybe—that will get both of you out of her place.

• *Examine your motives.* Here, from a decorated veteran of the sixties, is a short list of less-than-lovable reasons for taking a woman to bed: Sport, mercy, bother, relief, spite, convenience, proximity, conquest, old friends, boredom, curiosity, politics, job.

• *Assume responsibility for what you're doing.*

Moving In. A woman moves in figuratively long before she shows up with the extra stereo. Women come with a congenital ability to seduce with domestic subtlety: Suddenly your home life is decorated with all the ornaments of comfort—towels are dispatched to drawers, maybe, or there's a sudden defoliation of the refrigerator. That first hopeful fantasy of a life of homegrown ease starts to become a reality, and pretty soon you'd rather not live at all than live without it.

KNOW WHERE YOU'RE GOING TO LAND

Know what you expect from a woman before you fall in love with her. If you simply hope that falling in love with a woman will make you *feel* better, or if you just want somebody to nurse you through the illness of life, you're going to be disappointed. You're better off paying people to do work like that. Discounts are widely available.

Santayana's Revenge. Unless you're reading Dad's copy of this book, you have a personal history that is littered with the remains of old romances, like a collection of secondhand piñatas. By now, you should be able to see a pattern of some sort. Do you love women for six months, then run? Do women dump you after they get to know you well? Each of these sordid little affairs will have a critical, pivotal moment—the time you *insisted* she tell you that she loved you, the afternoon when she went on about her petty shop politics just one hour too many—when the worm of amorous angst rears its blind head and twists. Whatever went wrong before will go wrong again, unless you watch your step and try to change the normal course these things have taken before. Of course, you can't foresee everything, but if your romance is in reruns, you need a new writer.

THERE IS AN OBJECTIVE WORLD OUT THERE

In love? You know, you should try to get out more often. Bear in mind, for example, that there is no universal standard of beauty, and no matter how good-looking your sweetie is to you, to somebody else she's so-so at best. In your inebriated, druglike state, she's the most talented, the most intelligent, the funniest, most sensitive woman on the planet. But remember, your pals are out here, watching. And to us, she's just some girl laboring under your squidlike preoccupation. In fact—frankly? To us, she's your problem, not ours.

CHAPTER TWO

MODERN LANGUAGE

There you sit, wearing a solid-waste hairpiece, wondering how you could ever let three little words bring you so low. She said, "I love you"; she said you were swell. But then she dropped you; she said, "Go to hell."

What happened? Let's answer with a little anecdote. A guy gets out of the Navy, comes to visit a friend living in London. For three or four weeks, he thinks England's swell, a green and pleasant land. He meets a woman, she dumps him. Suddenly, the British Isles become a wet and brutish place, filled with nasal-twinged snobs. Finally, one day, he packs to go home. "You know what it is?" he says to his friend. "It's their language. I can't understand them. It's like they don't speak English here."

Life in the land of women is a little like that. You meet a woman, think everything's fine, then one day realize you were talking to a creature from another species, somebody who made noises similar to English, but didn't really speak your language at all—except when she wanted to be absolutely, fully understood, like when she said those three little words, "Go to hell."

And so it passes with every man. Eventually, we all come to see that the life span of modern love is calibrated in three-word soundbites that mark, with complete clarity, the beginning, middle, and end of any entangled alliance:

- Whatcha doin' Friday?
- I love you.

- Slower, harder, faster.
- Here's the key.
- Please marry me.
- Let's go shopping!
- Honey, I'm pregnant.
- Junior needs braces.
- Gimme a beer.
- We never talk.
- I need space.
- Gotta work overtime.
- Just a friend.
- I want alimony.

The Law of Linguistic Limitation. Strange, isn't it, how the really important things in a romance can all be hitched to little word troikas? Why is this? *Because any conversation longer than three words between a man and a woman is subject to wildly different interpretations and meanings, leading to the same old conflicts and arguments.*

INTRO TO GIRL-TALK 101

We must speak to them—women, that is—for they are here, amongst us, and they can't *stand* to be ignored. But words are the tools of misunderstanding, and so to be able to speak with women, we must first know their language.

The History of Women and Language

There are two distinct linguistic families from which all modern Western tongues are descended. One is Indo-European. The other is girl-talk. Indo-European gave us Greek, Latin, and Esperanto. Girl-talk gave us Gloria Allred, Joan Rivers, and prime-time television.

Girl-talk is a difficult tongue to master. Women, philologically, are the Magyars of our race, speaking a language so obscure that not even other women can always be sure of what they're talking about. Hence, "What do you mean by that?" is the reply given by most women to almost anything said to them by almost anyone.

• The exception: "Oh, grow up," which is what women say to men when men don't behave as women wish them to behave.

• Sweet-talk: Remember, language reflects culture, and all foreigners love a good diplomat.

Whatever Happened to Man-Talk?

This language-thing poses a special problem for men who, for whatever reason, find themselves faced with the desire or necessity of talking with a woman, since the linguistic tradition employed by men is less inclined to nuance than the language used by women.

To digress, this linguistic distinction is a relatively new development. Man-talk finds its origins in the primal, constipational grunts our forebears employed to warn each other of impending woolly-mammoth-doom. The onward march of civilization has expunged much of man-talk from the speech patterns of our gender.

A very great deal of the language used by men has been polluted by long years of service to politics, poetry, philosophy, phishing, and philandering—all enterprises requiring, to various degrees, a certain practicality of lingo. Today, if one man asks another, "Do you have a headache?" the second man is likely to answer yes or no, since the second man knows, instinctively, that to answer otherwise would be to open a line of uncalled-for discourse. A woman, of course, would answer the same question with another one, but more aggressively put. "How did *you* know I have a headache?" she would ask, vexed. Drug companies market pain pills with advertising based on this simple distinction. There is a great deal of subtext to a rejoinder such as that one, but the main thing is this: If a woman wants to talk around the subject, she speaks quite bluntly and directly about something else, something quite beside the point.

Alas, when men talk to women, they have no alternative language behind which they might hide their fears, aggressions, prejudices, or motives. But when women talk to men, the words they speak have been turbocharged with subtle meanings and delicate twists. When women speak, the crystalline ring of girl-talk wafts on the air.

There are exceptions to this assertion, of course. One is found in the guttural growls of the big, weeping Injun whom Robert Bly thinks lives in the soul of every Fuller Brush man. Another more prevalent exception may be found in the occasional livestock noises some men make at passing women in the apparent hope that a really well-delivered bark or howl will encourage a beautiful babe to remove much of her clothing right there on the boulevard.

HOW NOT TO TALK TO WOMEN

> *His talk was like a stream, which runs*
>   *With rapid change from rocks to roses:*
> *It slipped from politics to puns,*
>   *It passed from Mahomet to Moses;*
> *Beginning with the laws which keep*
>   *The planets in their radiant courses,*
> *And ending with some precept deep*
>   *For dressing eels, or shoeing horses.*
>
>   *—Winthrop Mackworth Praed*

Little is known anymore about Winthrop Praed, who, until he died of consumption in 1839, looked fair to be prime minister of England one day. Of this, however, we are certain: He shows us how *not* to talk to women, most of whom prefer their men to make conversation that is brief and to the point, unless it is about them. We share this trait, by the way, but we put it in abeyance, provided there's a damned good punch line.

Consider Their Feelings. If you want to get it right, bear in mind that women are extremely sensitive—not necessarily to the feelings of others, as myth has it, but rather to their own feelings. That is, a woman will happily, sometimes unwittingly, cut you to ribbons, and she will viciously attack other women without regard to extenuating circumstances. But every woman, no matter how little she cares about the feelings of others, is extremely sensitive about the things that you say to *her*.

Hola, Howdy, Hey. For example, the simple word "hello," uttered to a woman, can take on radically different meanings, depending on whether it is

   a. shouted out the window of your car to her in her ragtop Mustang on a sunny afternoon on the Hollywood Freeway, or
   b. spoken cheerfully to her as she passes on a busy sidewalk, or
   c. muttered softly to her as she enters the men's room because the line for the women's room was unmanageable, or
   d. whispered to her with awe as you stare directly at her breasts, or
   e. said straightforwardly as part of a traditional greeting ritual.

In every instance, no matter which words—if any—she actually speaks in response, the meaning of her language is always the same: "What do you mean by that?"

TEN THINGS TO NEVER TELL YOUR WIFE OR GIRLFRIEND

In a relationship, everything you say will be held against you until the day you die. Note well, then, these ten things to never tell your wife or girlfriend, presented in random order:

1. *"You know, maybe you'd like working out. Just to loosen up. Really."*
Or any variant on the why-don't-you-lose-a-few-pounds theme. For many men, a tryst is not only an opportunity to play John Simon, it's an occasion for subordinating the woman they're with in order to camouflage their own insecurities. Besides, women always know *exactly* what their bodies look like: If she's fat, she knows it; if she's skinny, she knows that; and if her ass is flat, she's already spent a lifetime twisting like a living pretzel in front of full-length mirrors. She doesn't require your evaluation of her failings. She already knows what they are.

While most men think of life as a sort of come-as-you-are party, body-wise, women learn early in life to pay attention to the odd things their bodies do. So, if puberty for boys is a race against the clock to get laid, puberty for girls is an episode of "Bringing Up Kafka," where the normal assumptions of life are given over to science fiction. Thus, by the time a woman shows up in your bed, she knows her physical shortcomings better than she knows herself. Even a very beautiful woman's vision of herself is clouded by her constant awareness of whatever bump or blemish may have obsessed her.

And by the way, this rule of downplaying your lover's body goes for *any* pronouncements on the physically obvious. If you say to your wife or girlfriend, "My, you have tiny breasts," she's likely to say to you, "What's that cute, little, teeny worm-thing you got down there, tucked behind that washer lint in the corner of your Jockeys?"

2. *"Honey, toss me that roll of toilet paper, would you?"*
Privacy is an aphrodisiac. Foster it, nurture it, insist on it.

3. *"Why can't you do anything right?"*

An unfair accusation of poor performance is the last refuge of an incompetent. She's your sweetheart, not the hired help, so this comment is doubly insulting if it follows her effort to do something you really ought to have done yourself, and it's triply insulting if it comes as a result of simply doing something *differently* from the way you would do it.

As a rule, if you see only her failings, it's because you have chosen to ignore her successes. Consequently, she may soon choose to ignore you altogether. Even if she sticks around, talking to your wife or girlfriend as if she were the lawn-jockey is not particularly attractive.

4. *"Hey, you, lend me a few bucks for my car payment, okay?"*

Despite the stylish movement away from gender burden, one of the very few true measures of a man is how well he meets his responsibilities. Men must make their own way, trying never to be a trial to those around them—and especially not to their emotional dependents. Some things will never change, and this is one: A man's job is to earn his own keep and provide for those he loves. If he fails at this, he succeeds at nothing.

- An ancillary never-say: "Hell, I got kids I never even seen." Nor, presumably, supported.

5. *"Dammit, honey, I guess you have the right to know: I got drunk two years ago at the office and did it to Barb in shipping and now I feel just like hell, guilty and miserable, so please forgive me, sugar babe, and it won't happen again. I mean it. Swear."*

Our lesson here has to do with telling lies, and the sense of it is this: Every lie you tell your wife or girlfriend will eventually come back to haunt you. Every single one. Without exception. Bank on it. The next time you wish to try to get away with a little lightweight infidelity, think of the world as a small town where all the other citizens are your brothers-in-law. So it's only a matter of time before the woman in your life learns everything you do and say, everything you think and feel. When cornered by your sweetie with the horrible truth of your spend-thrift, indolent, selfish ways, she already has the truth in her pocket, so admit all and hope for mercy. There are times when life with a woman is like spending the night in the Chinese police station of your mind, where the bright light of truth shines full on your sweaty brow, where to lie is to die, and where honesty is always the best policy.

But, for crying out loud, *never volunteer*. If, for example, somebody sneaked up behind you and thwacked you in the head with a big, dumb, stupid idea about cheap sex and the next thing you knew, you were lost on the dark avenue of lust, keep it to yourself. Announcing an infidelity is invariably something people do to make themselves feel better, and is always at the added expense of the person who has been betrayed, and who is then expected to offer absolution. Ignatius of Loyola, founder of the Jesuits, knew all about this. In his *Spiritual Exercises* he describes the circle of sin, despair, and absolution, which, with some modification, works something like this:

- You sin,
- you feel horrible and guilty, and, in your pain and anguish,
- you seek absolution.
- It is granted, and you feel joyful and exuberant. In fact,
- you feel so *damn* good, you go out and sin again.

Loyola was a saint. Your wife or girlfriend probably isn't.

You get what you pay for, atonement-wise, so suffer long and in silence. Telling your girlfriend about your stupid indiscretions is looking for an easy way out of a situation you got yourself into. (See Chapter Six, "Modern Mayhem and Cheating Hearts.")

- An ancillary never-say: "Gotta work late, sweetheart."

a. "Gotta work late, sweetheart" is a nice thing to say to your wife or girlfriend if you really are working late, since it demonstrates not only your sense of duty, but also your affection and consideration. And if you want to be believed, offer to pick up some Chinese food on the way home. However:

b. "Gotta work late, sweetheart" is a stupid thing to say to your wife or girlfriend if you're unemployed.

c. "Gotta work late, sweetheart" is an evil thing to say to your wife or girlfriend if, instead of working late, you are really going to go down to Bob's Palace of Topless Yahoos n' Brews to spend the night pouring liquor down the throat of a waitress to make her blind to your utter lack of honor and integrity, and hence more willing to help you roast your faithless weenie.

6. *"How strange that we should be together. I mean, you're not really my type."*

By "type" we're not talking about a dissimilar sense of humor or a divergent view on the appropriate use of Naugahyde or anything else having to do with character, intelligence, or personality. Men deal exclusively in superficialities when it comes to pigeonholing women they've known for less than, say, a year. So score bonus points if, having told her she's not your type, you then proceed to describe in detail just *precisely* what your type looks like, and get a free game if none of the details match the physical characteristics of your woman. Almost always, this sort of thing is done in the same insecure spirit as pointing out your lover's physical shortcomings (see above). Most women have an obvious, generic response to this sort of comparison shopping: "Why don't you go find somebody more your type?"

7. *"Without you, I'm nothing."*

There are probably better ways to instill in your wife or girlfriend a healthy sense of respect for you than to continually confess and whine about your weaknesses and how much you depend on her. This sort of thing is, of course, gross manipulation, a way of putting a price on any sudden decision on her part to blow you off. Naturally, lots of women think reducing you to nothing is a very cheap price to pay to be rid of someone with so little self-esteem, for here's a simple truth: Women are Darwinists; they *despise* weaknesses in men. Women want you to be strong, like Dad, so they don't have to be strong for both of you.

- An ancillary never-say: "My father never told me he loved me."

So? Sue him. Then get a life. The statute of limitations for real or imaginary psyche-crimes committed by unfeeling dads expires at the age of majority, after which time women have the right to expect men to assume responsibility for their own misfortunes. Self-absorbed women especially take this sort of thing poorly, since, after all, they are already the center of their own universes; they are adept at inventing excuses for their own misbehavior and neuroses, and they aren't apt to be sympathetic to you when you try to milk the same psychological cow, mostly because they're busy being mad at their moms. Egocentric women hate competition.

- A tangentially related never-say: "I'm sorry."

Civility is a swell thing, and good manners are always in style. But make sure your apologies are for genuine transgressions, not for the state of your own, personal, cosmic odiousness. Men who wimp around begging for reassurance often live lives of a certain desperate, celibate charm.

- A secondary never-say, applicable mostly to first dates: "I think you'd make a wonderful mother." Also: "I wonder what our children would look like." Also: "I think it's sexy to think of you pregnant."

In the sequence of early dates that constitute the opening gambits of courtship (see Chapter One, "Modern Love"), the primary focus should always be on cause, not effect. Besides, announcing not only undying love but also lifelong entanglements to a virtual stranger is one of many ways we help disappointment gain purchase in our lives.

8. *"You had a friend named Cheryl? Funny, I once had a girlfriend named Cheryl. She was really beautiful, had legs you wouldn't believe. God, she was sexy. I wonder if it's the same woman?"*

This really happens: Boy meets girl, boy likes girl, girl moves in, and suddenly one day three months into the relationship, boy finds there are two things he absolutely cannot refuse to talk about. One is his old cars ("I used to drive a Lamborghini"); the other is his old girlfriends ("When I was at Syracuse I used to date a go-go dancer named Cheryl Lamborghini who knew Lindsay Wagner personally"). When men play this part of their tape, women roll their eyes and wait for him to cue up "Nothing Compares 2 U." Women don't care; they don't want to know about your ancient case of crabs or your swinging bachelor past. In fact, the *only* thing women want to know about your old girlfriends is whether or not they gave you herpes simplex or any other still uncared-for STD—and whether or not you're still seeing any of them. The old girlfriends, that is.

9. *"Why is that guy looking at you? Did you smile at him? Huh? Did you? You did, didn't you! I knew it! Whore."*

Jealousy is really the outer limit for most women, who, unlike most men, don't see it as a measure of affection, but rather as a demeaning, highly insulting manifestation of insecurity. Of course, if it's your wife or girlfriend who's the jealous one, then it's not jealousy at all, it's justified suspicion, based on a long history of *very possible* misbehavior, and the way you looked at that woman in black Spandex last week, and an almost-forgotten confession on your second date about your misspent youth.

Men set themselves up in this regard far more often than women do, usually by trying to live one fantasy or another. Some guy will tell his wife or girlfriend that maybe a threesome would be exciting, and presto! one afternoon there's the UPS man wearing those regulation brown UPS boxer shorts making a delivery right there in bed with the guy's wife, who looks up innocently and says, "Gee, Albert, this was a great idea you had."

10. *"I do."*

Well, okay, it's not that you should *never* say this to your girlfriend. It's just that you should think long and hard first so you only have to say it to your girlfriend *almost* never. Like once, to be exact.

FIVE THINGS A SMART MAN WILL TELL HIS WIFE OR GIRLFRIEND

1. *"I love your body."*

As noted above, women are always aware of their physical shortcomings. Alas, the converse does not hold: Women apparently do not have a firm fix on their *positive* physical attributes. Hence, any discussion about the way your wife or girlfriend looks should always include your comment that you *love* her body, that you adore it, that it's what you think about all day and dream about all night, that you think it's so much more than just a cheap way to keep her chin off the floor. Women can't hear this enough. "I love you" is fine, but for most women under age eighty, "I love your body" is better.

2. *"Listen to this."*

> *When you are old and grey and full of sleep,*
> *And nodding by the fire, take down this book,*
> *And slowly read, and dream of the soft look*
> *Your eyes had once, and of their shadows deep;*
> *How many loved your moments of sad grace,*
> *And loved your beauty with love false or true,*
> *But one man loved the pilgrim soul in you,*
> *And loved the sorrows of your changing face.*
> *And bending down beside the glowing bars,*
> *Murmur, a little sadly, how Love fled*
> *And paced upon the mountains overhead*
> *And hid his face amid a crowd of stars.*
>   *—William Butler Yeats*

Reading aloud heart-poems like this one is a gently seductive gesture. Never mind what the poem means. Might be a downer or something. But it just sounds *great* read right out loud, especially if you can work in a little crack of emotion after the "pilgrim soul" bit.

If this is too caloric, try something from *Slow Hand,* an anthology of women's erotica edited by Michele Slung, and filled with every wonderful thing you need to win a woman's heart, but only if you're sneaking up on it from behind.

3. *"I got a raise."*

Here's a phrase that's never out of season, one that rings sweet no matter when it's spoken. If the subject is employment, bear in mind that while most women aren't mercenary wenches, every woman sees a new dimension of power in a lad who's pulling his own weight. Remember, a man's job is often the most attractive thing about him—why do men think it's jake to lust after women with giant breasts, but horrible for women to lust after men with giant paychecks?—and his success only adds luster to his image.

4. *"Let's get out of here."*

Lovers often find that the humdrum grind of daily life together can quickly suppress the spark that brought them together in the first place. But we've already warned you about traveling romance, so choose your itinerary with care. A romantic weekend for two in the country will reinforce that us-against-them, two-hearts-alone-in-a-heartless-world theme that, to you, seems to help make your love affair seem so incredibly unique. But a weekend for two at a Werner Erhard seminar or a regional NOW convention won't.

5. *"Thanks very much."*

Appreciation of small things, good manners, and gestures of recognition all help intensify a woman's feeling of worth. A wife or girlfriend taken too long for granted will not only go away, she'll go away mad.

HOW TO TALK DIRTY

The distinction between vocal and oral sex is a fine one, depending mostly on what you're doing while you're talking. For example, discourse takes on a wonderful dimension if you sometimes remember that silence is a virtue, or that you can do a lot of talking with your hands.

Sometimes, though, you just have to find the right words. For instance, as we noted in *The Modern Man's Guide to Life,* there are people—and you know who you are—who just can't go to the game without some sort of color analysis going on in the background. A good play-by-play man can heighten the general excitement of the match, provided a few rules are observed.

• ***Keep your opening remarks vague and nonspecific:*** "I'm just happy to be here," "We're going to give it our best shot," "I'm excited just to be a part of this." There are a million ways of saying this. Choose one.

• *As the play unfolds, use your skills at color commentary to keep the momentum going.* Avoid insipid variations on "This is as good as it gets," however, since your wife or girlfriend assumes it better get a *lot* better than this pretty quick. Don't be afraid of lapses in your commentary, but if you feel silence is dampening the proceedings, try "I love your body" (see above), a never-fail line.

• *In the heat of the action, a little straightforward play-by-play will work wonders.* Simply announce, in an urgent but straightforward way, exactly what you're doing to her, along with a scattering of hints about what to look for next. Use the most direct language you can imagine and eschew euphemisms: Telling your wife or girlfriend that you're doing "the old in-out" may not excite her. And don't take this ballpark metaphor very far, either. Your wife or girlfriend really doesn't want to hear you yell, "Going, going, going, *boom!* Hey, it's outahere!"

Another, related approach is to follow a straight linear progression, as in (a) I'm going to do this; (b) we're doing it now; (c) we did that and it was really something. The lad who submitted this tender tip said it was "like doing a TV show about fishing."

• *Hush.* Postgame, go from being a grizzly to being a stuffed bear. Let your wife or girlfriend do the talking for a change. Above all, don't ask questions—especially ones that call for her to make an analysis of the plays, since, unlike other ball games, sometimes it isn't over when it's over. Plus, it's a long season.

THE MOTHER-TONGUE

Women are born with the ability to pronounce simple words in a tone so terrifically compelling that they *must* be obeyed. It is the sound God gave mothers to use to discipline their children and to keep them from walking under busses, but, like any good thing, it can be turned to evil ends.

An illustration: After dinner one Christmas Eve in the early seventies, a group of nine adult men were gathered in the kitchen of a large, rambling apartment in New York City. In the far-off living room, their wives, girlfriends, and children were sitting quietly around the tree, and maybe somebody was reading a story, but that's not for sure. The important thing was that the women and children were far away when the violence broke out.

There were five guys standing between the refrigerator and the door, and four more guys standing next to the sink. Without any provocation, one of the men—a magazine editor, as it happens, who was standing next to the sink—tore off a paper towel, soaked it under the tap, and threw it at a man who a few years later wrote the script for a very popular movie about college screwoffs. It hit him in the forehead and stuck there, like a vicious skin tumor. He peeled it off and threw it back, but it went wild! and hit another man, a nervous travel writer, who retaliated by throwing it back. The travel writer threw like a girl, all wrist, and succeeded only in hitting an innocent humorist. The guy standing next to the travel writer—a cartoonist, if memory serves—doused another paper towel, then another, and so did his sink-based brothers and you know the rest. It was probably the most fun the nine men had ever had as grown-ups and it went on for perhaps five minutes until a woman stuck her head in the kitchen door, catching everyone by surprise, and said, "Sean!" *just like a mom.*

The nine men dropped their wet paper towels and went to midnight Christmas services and then took their children home to bed.

Five years later, I heard Sean had dumped the woman, but by then it was too late.

HELLO? HELLO?

Talking with women is fine. Listening to them is better.

Women frequently complain that men are so preoccupied with what they are going to say next that they completely miss what is being said to them. Women are irritated at having to say everything twice, of course, so it helps to remember that most times a woman says something to you, she's said it before. You just weren't listening.

BODY LANGUAGE

While men sit with their knees apart and talk staring into space, women sit with their legs crossed and play eye-tag all night long. For men, conversation has a thrilling dimension of confrontation. For women, conversation has a reach-out-and-touch-you sincerity, a fullness of feeling most men would like to avoid.

The Right Moves. It pays to know what a woman is saying with her body because she may be articulating what anthropologists call presenting behavior. You can tell a woman is concealing some attraction to you, for example, if she faces you, arches her body backward, reaches up and runs her fingers through her hair while groaning softly, softly traces the contour of her figure, pausing briefly at her breasts, then tells you she's glad to make your acquaintance while her eyes are still half-closed and her whole body is trembling in ecstasy.

The men's version of this is a little more subtle, and usually involves characteristics that are seen only on a first meeting and never again: Listening intently, long eye-to-eye smolders, boyish grins. Smart guys resurrect these manipulative gestures on special occasions—anniversaries, birthdays, and the like.

WHAT WOMEN SAY WHEN THEY SPEAK OF SEX

Women are not terribly forthright when they have to talk about you-know-what. Especially compared to men, whose language has been richly embroidered with a certain, shall we say, adolescent feverishness, women's sex talk drifts into labored euphemisms that seem to lack much imagery. For example:

• The Lexicon of Male Genitalia

Women's terms	Men's terms
It, that, thing, dick (if she wants to sound brazen), penis (if she's fairly serious), down there (if she's really serious), manhood (if she's a romance novelist).	Johnson, John Thomas, Willy, Wally, Burke, Jones, Orca, dolphin, old red, the redheaded stranger, Brontosaurus, one-eye, crank, throbber, shooter, spitz, little squirt, weenie, meat, meat whistle, sausage, salami, roast, tube steak, dick, member, prick, eel, worm, night crawler, snake, hog, Moby, train, love loco, dowel, love unit, hose, hydrant, skin flute, hairsplitter, rope, lizard, newt, the rocket, rifle, love gun, bullethead, howitzer ammo, love muscle, stick, log, rod, pudding, old puddinhead, pud, weasel, wing-wang, wong, dong, dingdong, wand, cock, rooster, banana, cucumber, big dill, bone, pecker, peter, router, Roto-Rooter, pipe, pole, tool, torpedo, Fat Man, Little Boy, Geraldo, choad, copperhead, love boa, love Scud, Saddam, the thing that wraps around my shoulders and still drags on the ground, wee-wee, and so on and on.

You get the idea. What's odd here is that the names men have for their own meaty members are not, as words by themselves, obscene, while many of the names men have for women's genitalia—as well as for the sex act—are.

HOW TO SAY HELLO TO A WOMAN

Don't:
Howdy; hiya, hiya; *enchanté,* woo-woo.
Do:
Hello.

Women like a straight-ahead approach when meeting a man for the first time, since their object is to find out as many salient facts about you as possible—straight or gay, single or married, employed or broke—and half-baked, clichéd wisecracks delivered with a nervous tremor in the vocal cords just get in the way. Men, alas, seem to lose their ability to articulate clearly when meeting a woman for the first time. Consequently, women talk to themselves while men mince around with banalities. He's saying something fatuous about his broker or his boat, while she's thinking: How do I feel about this guy? Does he make me feel good about myself? Is he the best for me he can possibly be? No matter what a woman is saying to you while she is being introduced, there's a simultaneous conversation going on between her and her feelings.

Men don't do this. Men move their thoughts to their shorts when they meet a woman. Says, "Hi"; thinks, *thigh.* If a man wants to get in touch with his feelings when he's meeting somebody new, he leaves a message for them to meet him in the men's room later.

Usually, introductions are a bust because of bad timing. After being introduced to a woman he finds attractive, it takes an average man as long as thirty minutes to regain control of the speech portion of his brain. Alas, often by the time a man has finally said "Hello," a woman has already said "Good-bye."

A Final Word About Language and Politics

Remember that for some women every sentence you utter can and will be held against you. This is especially true if the words you speak have a biological or sociological context. For many women, biology is politics.

Want to start a fight? One little word ought to be enough to do it. As if you needed the help, here's a short list of pump-action, all-purpose, twelve-gauge words:

- Mother
- Children
- Menstrual
- Work
- Clarence
- *Playboy*
- Sex
- Girl.

CHAPTER THREE

MODERN WOMEN AT WORK

Once, long ago, when working men would rise from their breakfast tables, kiss their wives and kids good-bye, and go to work, it was as much for the company (largely other men) as it was for the money (largely spent on the wives and kids). Men's lives were lived on the job as much as at home, and they would tirelessly joke that the trouble with women was you couldn't live with 'em and you couldn't live without 'em but, at work, at least, you could complain about it either way.

But things have changed. Maybe you still can't live with women and maybe you still can't live without 'em, but, if you're an average Joe, you *must* spend all day working with them, which is very much like living with them, *except no complaints are allowed.*

The appearance of women at work is not a new phenomenon, of course. If women hadn't gone to work during both world wars, men would have had to fight by yelling at each other long-distance. The *issue* of women at work, however, is of some measurable topical fascination, the subject of endless conflicting analyses, the predicate for professional female activists, and the basis of almost every new sitcom that backs up the networks' plumbing.

Suddenly, offices, factories, and shops are highly electrified arenas filled with oppressors and oppressed. The workplace is a warren of cubicles and closets where tense flirtations and secret romances live right next door to hurt feelings and rejection. The air is hot and damp with anger; memos and reports compete with tears and bad manners; danger lurks everywhere; personal ruin can be found in a curly hair on a Coke can.

MAKING A MOUNTAIN OUT OF ANITA HILL

We might as well talk about sexual harassment right off the bat, since the noise surrounding that issue is drowning out all rational conversation. A little background, maestro, please:

The Prohibition Impulse. As a social phenomenon, a rise in organized feminism—not the common political state of all women—has a cyclic pattern of recurrence, like ballroom dancing or economic recession. Each time they reappear, activist feminist movements are spawned by a pressing need to redress a social ill. A handful of theorists perform a valuable function in articulating the problem and focusing attention on it. But each time, specious organizations soon spring up in an effort to legislate their version of nice behavior.

For example, the last time women organized for justice, we got universal suffrage, which was a very good thing. But an alliance of women's groups and religious zealots also gave us Prohibition, an attempt to use the law to make men behave the way politically correct women of the time wished them to behave, and that was a very bad thing.

This time around, we got antidiscriminatory labor and social statutes, and that's a very good thing. But we also got a new batch of women's organizations, and now we're being threatened with censorship and, in the case of sexual harassment, once again with laws that are intended to make men behave the way politically correct women wish them to behave, and that's not so good.

• *Sexual harassment, either as described by the law or in practice, is meaningless to reasonable men,* at least as a fixed concept. Ask five hundred people what constitutes sexual harassment, and you'll get five hundred answers. In fact, during the Thomas hearings, that is precisely what the media did. They asked over and over again what constitutes sexual harassment. They devoted hours and hours to the subject. "This is great," said one female activist on television. "This is a national teach-in."

Trouble is, nobody learned anything. Nobody knows with any more clarity now than they did before what sexual harassment is, *exactly*. "We can't say in all cases a hug is sexual harassment or an invitation for a date is sexual harassment," Fraeda Klein, a consultant who organizes sexual harassment training programs for businesses, told the *Washington Post* in the middle of all the Hill-Thomas hoopla. "But what we can say is that in some cases it is sexual harassment. We have to know how the recipient feels."

In 1991, a federal appeals court ruled that an action which a "reasonable man" might find inoffensive may in fact be recognized as sexual harassment—but only by a "reasonable woman." That means that sexual harassment is a crime that reasonable men *cannot* recognize before the fact, that it is a crime that can *only* be discovered by women, and even then, presumably, only by a specific woman, since it hinges on an unwanted sexual advance, which, under some other circumstance, might be either a wanted sexual advance or no sexual advance at all, in which case, a reasonable woman wouldn't mind—unless she wanted it to be a sexual advance and it wasn't, in which case she might get mad.*

Now, art is something you recognize when you see it. But the law ought to lack such a margin for self-expression. And as law, this certainly won't work—and certainly not as a crime the mere accusation of which can destroy families and marriages, and ruin careers. If Gennifer Flowers had charged Bill Clinton with sexual harassment instead of sexual conquest, the Bill and Hill show would still be playing Little Rock.

The hysterical effort to codify niceness is ultimately futile, of course.

---

*In France, typically, things are even more confusing. A man can be put in jail for sexual harassment in France. Yet, in a recent survey, a full 20 percent of women surveyed said they didn't think a potential employer asking them to disrobe constituted sexual harassment. No wonder France is the nation that invented sex comedies.

It's precisely this sort of thing that elevates the level of misunderstanding and mistrust between men and women, especially since some feminists have sought to put "sexual harassment" on a par with rape—something that rape victims must find grotesque. Imagine if "sexual provocation" to gain a personal or professional advantage—that certain glance, that plunging neckline, that very short skirt, those too-high heels, that coy invitation for coffee—were a statutory offense that could be comprehended *only* by reasonable men, and even then, only by those who were annoyed by such behavior.

• *Men get it, all right.* Back a politically correct woman into a corner on this subject, and, bereft of logical argument, she'll eventually let fly with one of the most intellectually indolent phrases of this brain-dead century: She'll tell you that men "just don't get it."

She'll be wrong, of course. Reasonable men recognize that genuine sexual harassment actually involves three substantially different transgressions, namely:

• *Assault.* It's assault if a man reaches inside a female colleague or subordinate's blouse to see if her heart's in the right place.

• *Extortion.* It's extortion when a man says to a female colleague or subordinate, "Give me the world's greatest sexual experience right now, or tomorrow you'll be out of here."

• *Bad Manners.* It's bad manners when a man says to a female colleague or subordinate, "Nice hooters, hon," or whines for a date, or plays Siskel and Ebert with *LongDongophobia.*

Assault and *extortion* are crimes everyone understands. You can go to the slammer for that stuff, and it would serve you right.

Bad manners . . . well, that's something else. Everybody understands bad manners, too, but vulgarity, bad breeding, and coarseness are part of life in a particularly brutal age, and they aren't gender-specific. By and large, even jerks understand when they're being rude, and if they don't, there's certainly nothing impolite in telling them so. In normal circumstances (if, for example, offices weren't laboratories where imaginative sex crimes were being created), people guilty of egregiously rude behavior—whether it's making stupid comments to colleagues or running around the office with your hand under your arm making fart noises— would be warned, reprimanded, or fired, and indeed such is often the case. A management that is stupid enough to permit widespread rudeness isn't likely to stay in business long, and if a business allows actual criminal activity—assault, for instance—between workers to go unpunished, it can be held liable. But it's impossible to try to legislate the symptoms of good breeding, like proper manners. We live on the Planet of Rude People.

Women, of course, are as accomplished as men at manifesting bad manners or committing extortion, and assault is not a specifically masculine trait, as any child welfare officer can attest.

Bad Talk

Rudeness and other violations of civility contribute to the real crime in this situation—bad communication between the sexes. The feminist view of what constitutes sexual harassment can also be seen by reasonable people as a simple failure to communicate across gender lines. Women react to men, sometimes accurately. Men react to women, sometimes accurately. But most of the time, something's going to go amiss, especially when there's a deep undercurrent of *potential* sexuality, and a decided lack of perspective or even humor.

Here's the News. Women really do seek to gain the attention of men. Shocking, yet true: Some women—maybe nobody you know personally, alas, but *some* women—actually hope the right guy *will* initiate a conversation that will lead, ultimately, to a very badly wanted sexual advance. Sexual provocation and sexual harassment are sometimes officemates. (This revelation isn't really a secret: During the Thomas-Hill coverage on CNN, the Senate hearings were repeatedly interrupted by a Revlon commercial that featured beautiful, scantily clad women and a sound track that repeated the refrain: "Shake your body.") Sex is *everywhere* in this culture. It is a vital, engrossing, transcendent, sometimes charming fact of our common lives. It's not only on TV, in the movies, on the radio, and in art and literature, it's also in Bible camps, under the bleachers, and on top of the Great Smokies. It's at the post office, down by the old mill stream, in stores near you. Is it surprising that it's also at work?

Reasonable men—normal chaps innocent of assault, extortion, or bad manners—go to work, sense sex in the air, and, from time to time, react to it. Usually, the result is either a bad gag, a half-mumbled pleasantry, a nervous laugh, or an extremely well-oiled dinner invite. Sometimes, the result can be an unwanted sexual advance. But throughout the history of our species it is men's common experience that *most* of their sexual advances—of any sort, and no matter how innocuous, or even subconscious—prove to be unwanted sexual advances. Men, perforce, are empiricists when it comes to experiments in sexual chemistry: It's all trial and error, with errors outnumbering successes twenty to one. By and large, men just hope that when rejection comes, it won't be extraordinarily painful. Certainly, they hope it won't come with an arrest warrant.

Maybe women have been right all along: We just don't talk. How did it get this bad?

The Secret Life of Men. The sexualization of the office was absolutely inevitable as an unprecedented number of women baby boomers came of working age. Relatively well-educated and prosperous, many rejected their mothers' examples and headed straight for the amusements of WorkWorld, where they hoped they might find the same rewarding life they were certain men secretly must be leading. Women see men playing the games men play, and they see men swallowing the fallacy of self-importance, and they want to taste it themselves. Women, of course, find no more meaning in work than do men, and so their irritation grows— along with their belief that something is being held back from them, some crazy rewarding *thing* that will make sense out of life. They think this thing is hidden around the office somewhere, and the more they fail to find it, the more they hate men for hiding it.

If women are prisoners of biology, so are men. For example, if women are defined by what they *are,* men are defined by what they *do.* This essential meaninglessness for men leads to an affection for diversion, which is why a bunch of guys invented work in the first place. Men know it's just a façade in the shade of which a guy can pleasantly pass his four score and ten.

FIVE JOBS WOMEN CAN DO BETTER THAN MEN, OR COULD DO BETTER THAN MEN IF THEY REALLY WANTED TO

1. Any professional, skilled, or semiskilled job that doesn't involve heavy lifting
2. Car or boat salesperson
3. Game show hostess
4. Mom
5. Topless go-go dancer in white thigh-high boots, with breasts that defy gravity and a tiny black lace G-string and innocent eyes blue as the sky smiling right at you

Also: Women are better than men at listening carefully during a conflict, keeping an open mind, understanding divergent points of view, and taking revenge.

Don't be threatened. We have our strong points, too:

FIVE JOBS WOMEN APPARENTLY CAN'T DO AS WELL AS MEN, NO MATTER WHAT THEY SAY

1. Broncobuster
2. Philosopher
3. Politician or Roto-Rooter operator
4. Interior lineman
5. Pope

Also: Men are better than women at Thai kickboxing, getting jokes, hanging out, poking fun, and working well with women.

HOW TO TELL YOU'RE WORKING WITH WOMEN

Evidence of female co-workers is easy to spot. Watch for these telltale signs:

- Small, *living* potted plants, often wrapped in ribbons.
- Silver foil balloons bearing innocuous slogans and cute little bears.
- Coffee cups with Garfield or Kathy cartoons on them.
- Gnomes, fawns, and other figurines that double as paper-clip holders.
- Lots of BREATHING ZONE signs.
- Lots of photographs and personal souvenirs on the wall, and lots of *really* personal things stuffed into desk drawers.
- Women also read the fine print on calendars, so holiday and seasonal decor is another surefire woman-worker indicator.

Around an office, men decorate, to abuse a word, either by hiring women to do the job or by a system that might be called random placement of artifacts—a burger wrapper on top of the file cabinet, a ticket stub from a ball game on the wall, maybe an old air freshener in the corner under the desk. Women, on the other hand, bring little bits of America right into their cubicles, which become light, airy, colorful places decorated with just a hint of Hallmark.

DANGEROUS WORK

One of the most demanding work environments for a man is one in which women dominate. Pleasant as it might seem to be the only man in an officeful of women, here's a reality checklist showing what you can expect:

- Raunchy talk.
- Unwanted sexual advances.
- Prying, personal questions.
- Stupid nicknames.
- The assumption that your shoulders were made to be cried on.
- An expectation that you will lift any heavy object or open any jar, anytime, without complaint.

THE LOOK OF A WORKING WOMAN

Until twenty years ago, millions of women dressed for work without thinking about much more than what they would wear. But when working women became part of a constituency, what they wore became a personal statement of some sort, and the morning routine got a little more complicated.

Until their recent emergence from the fashion-prole era, they wore the international uniform of Working Woman, which looked like somebody sent the contents of some guy's closet off for a sex-change operation. The basic garb was a cotton blouse; maybe a necktie sort of like a man's; huge, white athletic shoes that made a woman look like one of those toys kids can't knock over; and a dark gray, sometimes pin-striped suit with *enormous* shoulder pads that made her head look like a teeny afterthought. All over America, offices looked like the set of *Honey, I Shrunk Dick Butkus.*

Now, work looks like an oversexed bridge club. Women seem to have gained the confidence to dress like actual women, and, suddenly, working women look lovely, sometimes even sexy—an observation a careful man will keep very much to himself. The atmosphere is different, too. There's something slightly inebriating about walking into an office for a meeting where the air is rich with perfume and great-looking women are everywhere. Fat Ottoman Turks must have lived like this once, you think. To yourself.

DEFENSE, DEFENSE, DEFENSE, AND DEPORTMENT

Be careful how you deal with women as co-workers. Good manners never change: You should try your best to maintain a certain amount of polite deference and courtly behavior, even though some traditional gestures may have to be abandoned in favor of job security. Normally, for example, a well-mannered man might be expected to rise when a woman enters his office. If you do that with a working woman, she won't even ask you where you are going. She'll just take your place.

There are a few common-sense rules that should always apply, but have special relevance in the workplace:

• Ensure the safety and security of women at work—especially in dark parking lots and passageways.

• Discourage other men in your company from making lewd comments at women or in the presence of women.

• Avoid touching women in any way that you wouldn't touch a man.

• Do not allow women to feel slighted, patronized, or ignored in the normal course of business.

But you can't abandon gender distinctions completely, either.

• Women take most things personally: If it's nine o'clock and you're reading the paper and sipping coffee, you can't ignore a woman the way you would a male colleague.

• Always, in dealing with women, remember that the emotional factor is close to the surface, and that even the most tactless of women will not shrug off insensitivity the way men will.

• Men should know they must tailor their conversations, however subtly, to take women into account.

• Finally, remember not to expect to share an easy camaraderie with most women; don't yell, "Yo, Momma," across the floor at a woman. She may have to hear it all night at home.

The safest way to treat women at work is politely. Which is, of course, the same way you should treat them elsewhere.

FLIRTING WITH DANGER

Some women in positions of power—including bureaucrats with only momentary influence—make many men feel that the basis of most confrontations has to be caustic, flirtatious, coy, catty, or otherwise personal. Some women feel threatened by even the slightest confrontation—being asked for a clarification, for example. Men who refuse to abide by this constraint, or who simply don't recognize it, will find themselves dealt with summarily. One guy got demoted for writing a routine memo asking for a policy decision.

Women often turn what, for men, are conventional disagreements into personal conflicts. One now-famous Manhattan D.A., when told about a defense attorney's rather impersonal view of an aspect of a case she had prosecuted, began her rebuttal by sighing to a reporter, "It's so like Jack."

Personalizing conflict is highly efficacious for women, as anyone who ever had to argue with an aunt, mom, or sister will recall with some pain. Lowering conflict to a personal level allows for no rational response. It creates a sort of instant suspension of the rules and moves the debate onto an emotional plane, one that most women find more comfortable. (It must be noted, however, that this feminine conceit wasn't lost on Ronald Reagan, who adopted it in the course of his pivotal debate with Jimmy Carter, when he responded to one of Carter's policy statements by saying, "There you go again," which was the 1979 equivalent of, "You just don't get it.")

Women in positions of authority find it easiest to perceive their positions as embattled. For them, even though personalizing conflict doesn't resolve the conflict, it does often win the debate, and for them, that's often good enough.

POLITICAL ALLIES

Office politics is largely a matter of who knows what about whom and how that knowledge can be used. Because many women are geniuses at gathering and trading information, they have a huge advantage in the office games.

That's another good reason to live your personal life outside the office. Once you start circulating office memos on the end of your dick, you're looking for big trouble.

But *women are at least as trustworthy as men.* They're certainly more loyal. As a rule of thumb, you're better off trusting a woman co-worker than you are trusting a man. Men play to win. Women often play to tie. Or, put it another, less savory way: Many men go to work the same way they go to war. Most women go to work the same way they go to bed.

CAUTION: SEX AT WORK

The good news is, work is where all the women are. The bad news is, work is where all the women are. If you try to ignore the obvious, you'll appear ludicrous, since sex-neutral behavior is for automatons. You can pull it off for a while, but as a way of life, being the office eunuch is deeply unrewarding. Worse, people soon grow to distrust and dislike the utterly sexless amongst them. Those who try to make sexlessness an office policy only breed complaining *castrati* and dour, sere broads. The result is a hostile work environment, almost as though sexual harassment were the office policy.

Besides, despite all the fashionable hysteria about office sex of late, most people understand that work is the easiest—*and most dangerous—*place to meet a potential mate.

The reasons for workplace romances are obvious:

• You get a chance to know someone better than you would in most other circumstances, so you probably won't have to face any troubling surprises—like an armed boyfriend at the door—when you take her home.

• The conversation for the first few dates comes with a built-in cushion that nearly precludes awkward silences.

• The tension of a secret office liaison is a mighty aphrodisiac. As one professional noted, there's nothing quite as arousing as sex on the office broadloom.

If you get involved with a co-worker, make sure you understand the boundaries of permitted behavior (see Chapter One, "Modern Love"). This is a highly situational thing, of course, since in some offices, interdepartmental intercourse is just part of the big, bad world, while in others, it's grounds for derailing not just one career, but two. You can rely on instinct, but you should double-check with Personnel.

Romances with a subordinate are the junk bonds of office affairs—easy to get into, expensive to get out of. Unless it's love and marriage at first sight, be careful on the first night: When you get involved with your assistant or your secretary or your boss's secretary, you not only take on the high-risk burden of conducting a courtship at work, but also the higher-risk burden of one day having to end it. For no matter how hard you try to be scrupulously honest and aboveboard, when you end an office affair, the shit doesn't just hit the fan, it goes through the whole climate-control system.

One-night stands with co-workers are even worse, because no matter who seduced whom, somebody's feelings are going to be hurt, and it's more likely to be hers than yours. If she dumps you after a one-nighter, tough for you. If you dump her after a one-nighter, the whole apparatus of social policy comes down on you: Imagine how much she'll hate you. Imagine what she'll be thinking when she looks at you. Imagine the things she'll say about you to your co-workers. Imagine what she'll say about you to your boss. Imagine when she becomes your boss.

Sleeping with your boss finds many parallels in the real world. It's sort of like, say, driving to Las Vegas with all your kids' college money, walking into a casino, finding a roulette table, and putting the whole pile on 16. It's like falling in love with a really sexy, drop-dead-beautiful twenty-year-old Moonie. It's like stepping forward to catch the baby thrown out of the sixth-floor window of a burning building. Many men enjoy high-risk activities. Few enjoy looking for a job.

WHO'S ON TOP

Many men—especially those in service and information industries—can go through a large part of their careers laboring under the supervisory eye of a woman boss. These men know that just as women can make great friends, they can also make great bosses.

But when you find the exception to this rule, you know it right away. Bad boss-women can also make bitter enemies, tyrants who wear their insecurity with electric ostentation and who will kill you before they'll accept the responsibility for a mistake they made. They can be martinettes who rule without mercy and who play the game of work with a stubborn blindness toward concepts like fair play—"irrelevant" concepts they claim men learned in Little League.

There's also a bottom-line inscrutability about many women bosses, some silent acknowledgment that no matter *what,* you can never go to her and have a buddy-to-buddy chat. It's the same unreadable quality that helps women excel in office politics. After all, most men avoid getting up-close and personal with their bosses—or with anyone else. When, because of some family emergency or some similar catastrophe, men find themselves wailing the blues in the boss's office, and the boss is another man, the situation is dealt with expeditiously, with a tacit agreement that the encounter will disappear from the calendar of events almost instantly and will never be a part of permanent memory. Men don't deal well in the commerce of emotions, so your slobbering confessional isn't a convertible currency with a man. Not so with most women. That ill-advised flowering of your inner-self will become a part of your personal profile, a never-forgotten dimension of your personality that will always be part of the background noise of any future conversation.

There's another nuance here as well. During the seventies and early eighties, when men were trying to cry their way into women's hearts, women learned that overly sensitized men were wimps who cried all day and were useless all night. These days, if you really want to get a cold shoulder from a woman, any woman, just try crying on it.

If you're the boss, you're a lucky chap, since women as subordinates have the clever ability to organize all those troublesome details that men customarily, and often with disastrous results, overlook. Women, as mentioned earlier, are more loyal, more likely to afford you protection when you need it, make better co-conspirators, and are less likely to trade your approval for a cheap shot at a promotion. Hence, the good women who work for you should be treated like gold.

THE UNSPEAKABLE

There are a number of bizarre aspects to working with women about which we must never speak.

The Moon, Aunt Dot, the Time, the Curse. From time to time, you may walk into a co-worker's office, say "Howdy," and watch in bewilderment as she breaks down in tears. You will be well-advised not to notice this sort of emotional enthusiasm, doubtless a consequence of PMS or some other gender-specific inconvenience. Women will earnestly and repeatedly deny that menstrual stress influences their behavior, yet PMS is occasionally the basis for defending murderesses, and the women of America support a menstrually related drug industry worth hundreds of millions of dollars. There's a chance that a woman's behavior might be somewhat altered by biology. This is not news, of course. It is simply one of the great unspoken truths, that, if uttered, subject the utterer to ridicule, defamation, and possibly sudden loss of income.

Flirtation. Women often use flirtation, innuendo, coyness—sexual harassment, if you insist—to accomplish goals and achieve aims at work.

Eventually, this may become part of the hideous public debate over sex in the offices and factories of America, but smart men will wait until somebody else brings up the subject.

Intuition. An absolutely irrefutable feminine manipulation of logic. If it's your subordinate who is suddenly overcome with intuition, ask her to put her case on more verifiable grounds. If it's your boss who has the sudden stroke of intuition, say, "Go with it, chief."

THE BIG PROBLEM

The obvious reason for our current obsession with office sex, sexual harassment, sexual favors, and sexual possibilities is that apparently nobody's keeping busy. While the Japanese nip at our right leg and the Europeans go for our left, America's businesses, sucked into the distraction of what the rest of the world sees, quite rightly, as a relatively pubescent issue, are sweating over girl problems and boy troubles while trying to make sure nobody's feelings get hurt. Soon we'll be a nation of florists.

Too bad it's become so much trouble; in even its most subtle shadings, sex can be the Mrs. Dash of quarterly plans, client lunches, or a day on the assembly line.

FINALLY, NO GENERALIZATIONS

Any judgment of women—as co-workers or as anything else—tends to be overly generalized. Many women will argue vehemently that none of this pertains to them, that women are no different from men, that the only problem with men and women working together is men. Women say men are jerks. Men say women aren't nice guys.

But maybe women are right to a certain extent, at least about making sweeping claims. Generalizations really are unfair.

So these are the women to whom this handy tract does not apply:

- Margaret Thatcher.
- Jeane Kirkpatrick.
- Mother Theresa.

CHAPTER FOUR

MODERN COHABITATION

Here are the seven ages of Man: The big bang, toilet training, cowboys and Indians, Little League, body hair, work, and girls. Then you discover the facts behind religion.

The mileposts of our lives pass, for the most part, without much notice. But between girls and death, there's a world of trouble. This passage, shorter than it ought to be, but often longer than it needs to be, is the subject of great reflection by most men.

In fact, if life is a carnival, love is the house of mirrors. There are mirrors here to make you look fat and mirrors to make you look small and someplace a mirror to tell you that you aren't alone at all, that suddenly there's somebody else in the picture. A woman. At first you see her here, then you see her there. Then, one day, you see her everywhere. Where once you were a bachelor, now you're not. A woman moved in. She is Germany, you are Poland. But despite its superficial complexity, your situation is really a simple one: You made yourself a zealot, a true believer. You donated a sizable portion of control over your happiness to what you thought was a worthy cause, and now you're caught in a situation that will lead, step by step, to a happy ending. Or to hell.

HOW SHE GOT THERE

Cohabitation is not an act of God. Like LEDs and Lancias and many other things that we find attractive but beyond reasonable understanding, cohabitation exerts a mysterious pull on us. Hence, in viewing the intricacies of live-in love, there are a few important elements you should always keep in mind:

1. *You asked for it.* You did, didn't you? Come on, admit it. One way or another, you found, if you'll pardon me, an interesting wrinkle to your life sitting opposite you, on the far side of an expensive drink or across an office desk. And, one way or another, you said, "Excuse me, but do you want to come and hang out and watch TV and bring all your clothes with you?" And, one way or another, she said, "Sure thing, sailor."

2. *The invitation probably took the form of a dare.* Of course, much of courtship is only a sequence of frivolous dares, not much different from the ones you used to make in college with your buddies. You meet a woman, you like her, and before you have time to look seriously at the situation, you're *daring* her to get involved with you, betting against very good odds that she won't want to play the female lead in your miniseries. Do this ten or twenty times, and pretty soon, it's a lark. Then one day you get a taker, and despite the fact that it was only an idea, really, you know, just a passing thought, she came and she stayed put.

3. *Women are hallucinogenic.* For men, crippled with an inability to see past the love that beats in their boxers, reality in romance is highly elusive. When you meet a more or less appropriate woman, you look at her and say to yourself, "This is the girl for me." You forget that what you're really looking at is the amazing length of her leg, the waspish tuck of her waist. To you, these things look like the promise of home comforts or boon companionship or decent breeding stock. Whatever it is you see, you think it's the real thing, something so real, in fact, you just have to go to bed with it.

4. *Women play for keeps.* Women, on the other hand, don't kid around. Women know that the presentation tape most men play to reveal the story of their lives runs about eight hours or so. An interested woman will wait patiently through this gaseous epic and watch closely and sometimes listen. During this moment-out-of-time, while the guy's

tedious life story is going full tilt, women—then and there—decide whether they're serious or not. If they're serious, eventually they go to bed with the guy; if they're not, they still might go to bed with the guy, but they'll wonder why later. Because if they're serious, the first date is the start of a much longer adventure.

So while for a man the whole episode may come to a close before breakfast, for her it's just beginning.

SHE'S AN EXPERT

She Knows Something You Don't. In addition to the natural inclinations and instinctive skills provided in the Maker's gender option kit, your new significant other has surrounded herself with the lore of relationships since the first bloom of her sentiency. Most of what she reads, sees on TV, talks to her friends about—in fact, much of what she feels and thinks impinges to one degree or another on her relationships with others. She is much more aware than you are of the subtleties of romances and friendships. Moreover, she has lived a life secure in the infallible belief that sooner or later, she will be involved in a comitted relationship, probably the wedded sort. This is not to say that women are out to trap men into marriage or anything like that. It's just that a reliable relationship is part of the context of her future, something she expects for herself.

You, meanwhile, have been toying with the philosophical implications of upper body strength and the heretical rules of American League baseball and the obscure laws that govern the DNA-like helices of Sam Donaldson's career path.

The Result. At relationships, she's an expert, and you're an amateur. And thus it will always be. Sure, as a man about town, you may have a way with babes or whatever, but once you start cooking off the same gas meter, she's a general, and you're a raw recruit, a buck private, a stupid conscript in a two-man popular front for domestic bliss.

WHEN TO SHARE REAL ESTATE

Once upon a time, you could get a girl to go steady by giving her a large, cheap Mexican ring, something leonine with a red rhinestone in one eye. She'd wrap it in angora and wear it around her neck to show the world she was yours, by heck. No more. Going steady these days means an exchange of house keys, and serious dating has become a form of temporary matrimony.

If you're deeply in love with the incredible mother-of-your-unborn-child, cohabitation is likely to seem a logical move, and nothing anybody can say will sway you. Sometimes, though, you may find yourself involved with some woman who, while possessing clearly appreciable traits, falls somewhat shy of dream-girl status. How do you know when to make the move? And what should you watch out for?

• *Don't move in with her for any practical reason.* Don't, for example, move in with a woman you're dating because her apartment is closer to work, or because your lease is expiring, or because you think two can live as cheaply as one. They can't. Conversely,

• *Don't shelter the homeless.* Don't allow her to move into your digs because she has no other place to go.

The idea here is to avoid a situation in which cohabitation is simply a way to avoid a passing hassle. If you try to take the easy way in and out of this, you'll eventually reap lots more trouble than you bargained for.

• *Don't move out in order to move in.* Keep your flanks clear for a quick retreat. Cohabitation, after all, has many of the characteristics of marriage, and in some cities—in New York, for example, where a long-term lease has more value than a short-term romance—it's far easier to find a divorce lawyer than it is to find a new apartment. It follows, then, that

• *If possible, make it your place instead of hers.* Children can create an exception to this rule, however. If she has kids and she is well-settled, don't invite turmoil by uprooting her family.

• *Don't solicit failure.* Examine the financial and emotional cost of cohabitation. Do both of you live in one-room apartments? If so, will cohabitation require a new apartment or house? Do either of you have children? Romance can cloud clear thought; don't assume that everything will work out if the two of you can only be together. In fact, nothing will work out without great effort, and new problems will occur without warning.

• *Don't fight over decor.* No matter who moves in with whom, if the look of where you live is important to you, keep one room—even a common room, like a dining room or bedroom—to yourself. Don't expect more than one room, however, as women tend to become household imperialists, colonizing every room as a matter of right.

• *Don't confuse this with marriage.* Cohabitation came into fashion as part of the fallout of the sexual revolution. What we wanted was sex without fuss, and a marriage contract was not only a hassle, man, but, sooner or later, it also involved divorce, which was uncool. So the way we figured it, it was better to live with somebody for a while and then split up, no hard feelings, than it was to marry somebody for a while and then divorce. Didn't work that way. What happened is that you lived together for a while, married for a while, divorced, then lived together with somebody else for a while before you married *that* person. Then you got divorced again. According to the most recent national surveys, as many as 85 percent of cohabitating couples end up uncoupled and habitating quite separately. Seen in this light, cohabitation may be yet another excellent reason to not get married at all. (There are, of course, many other fine reasons for not getting married. For a complete rundown, see Chapter Five, "Modern Marriage.")

HOUSE RULES

The rules you live by as an unmarried couple can differ substantially from those you might follow if you were married. For example, if you marry a woman, you may decide you have an obligation to support her in domestic splendor if she chooses not to work. But if you're living with someone who is, perhaps, only a long-running date, the last thing you want to see is her taking up TV as a day job. Best bet: Decide in advance who pays for what and who does what. In fact, if you're the sort of fellow who worries much about this sort of thing, try to make these rules formal by putting them in writing, even if it seems awkward.

No matter what the nature of your entanglement, though, some rules are always in order—commonplace stuff, really, like conventional etiquette and all that. Remember, even if she moves into your place, it's her home, too, and you're intruding on her as much as she's intruding on you.

WHAT HAPPENED TO YOUR SOCKS

We're going to assume here that you have become involved with a woman, and she has decided to become involved with your real estate, rather than the other way around. With that in mind, we can look at a few of the wide variety of changes that take place when first you allow a woman into your cage.

• *How to find your socks.* They're in the drawer, where she thinks they're supposed to be. You might have had them in a drawer already, but it wasn't the right drawer. Only she knows which drawer is the right drawer, and it's never the drawer you think is the right drawer.

Don't take it personally. You might be the Tony Randall of your block, the neatest chap in town. But the order you've imposed on your corner of the cosmos is not the same as the order *she* wants to impose on it. So pots and socks move around; a chair appears; a cat comes or goes; the bathroom, once a chapel of quiet contemplation, becomes a superficial-maintenance garage, crowded with beauty tools and all-weather bath oil. Suddenly, you will discover you own Q-Tips.

• *Telephone conversations as a spectator sport.* You find yourself talking to your best friend on the telephone while she watches—stands right there and watches. Suddenly you hear yourself telling your pal one or two of the whoppers you once told her—maybe the imaginary time you and your chum saved beached whales or something—and your friend is mortified for you.

• *Long-distance conversations.* Women prefer conducting conversations while standing or sitting in rooms other than the room you occupy. When you hear your name called, you are expected to stop doing whatever you're doing, walk into the room in which she is standing or sitting, listen to her, respond, then go back to whatever you were doing.

• *Mom-talk.* From time to time, the woman with whom you are living will address you in sharp and condescending tones, similar to those used by some women newscasters and by moms when they wish to bring unruly ten-year-olds back in line; this odd style of speech is a congenital condition for some and a professional affectation for others.

WHAT MAKES WOMEN REALLY MAD

Women are burdened with the unshakable suspicion that *deep down we're all bad boys.* This conviction explains much female behavior, and, perversely, can even help us learn a little about ourselves.

The Personal History of Trouble. For instance, we are conditioned to assume the worst about ourselves. After all, living with women is not new to us. Most of us, for example, lived with Mom for a while, and so we all know what's number one on our agenda: Do *anything* you can to stay out of trouble. That doesn't mean you can't get in trouble; it doesn't mean you can't cause trouble, laugh at trouble, or say trouble is your middle name. It just means you can't get caught. Because staying out of trouble means you don't get yelled at or put on probation or sent to your room—or worse, to a motel room.

Mostly, the things that cause women to get mad at men are things that probably didn't or wouldn't take place, but *might.* Women are mad at us because we *might* play poker with the rent money, or spend a paycheck on a new spinning reel, or drag the carcass of a dead deer in the kitchen door, or rediscover coeds. They have a point: We *might*. Men aren't 100 percent stupid; but they know they carry this inherited stupid-gene, and it makes them feel guilty, even when they don't do anything wrong. Because they *might*. As a consequence, men have given women the moral edge, and must, if they would avoid conflict, act in such a way as to not cause suspicion, even if their behavior is exemplary.

- Phone home frequently.
- Eliminate unexplained absences.
- Don't change your socks twice in one day.

Remember: You can trigger an instant argument by simply varying your daily routine. Although sometimes, it's worth the fight.

ANGER AND GUILT

Since women can get mad just *thinking* about how bad men are, this anger has social and personal implications. We'll deal with the social stuff later. Right now, let's deal with the woman in your face.

It's not that she's mad *this instant*. It's that she could be any minute. To you, this is a precariousness that is itself disruptive. To her, it's a 'tude, and it helps her keep her equilibrium, and, since you don't want an out-of-kilter woman running around the house, you are better off if you can help her maintain her incipient anger. *To successfully live with a woman, you must meet her expectations of your guilt without exceeding them.* This is Lawson's Rule of Good-Bad-but-Not-Evil Behavior. If you are insufficiently guilty, you will be suspect. If you are actually guilty, you will be killed, probably by an unarmed lawyer.

Presumed Guilty. In family court, men are presumed guilty, even by other men, and women are presumed innocent, especially by other women. In fact, one of the reasons men try so hard to stay out of trouble is that they *themselves* presume they must be guilty, what with that constant self-threat of possible bad behavior. Besides, why else would women be yelling at them all the time?

PATTON'S AXIOM

The point of all this is that it is absolutely essential that, from time to time, you conduct your daily life without explanation or apology. Assuming that you are trying your best to live up to your commitments and responsibilities, you are right to react angrily to constant demands for explanations. Occasionally, women will mask these demands as a request for "communication," but don't be fooled. There's a difference between conversation and explanation.

Women and Silence. While women often complain that men don't open up enough, they can do a pretty good job of clamming up, too. A soundbite of the familiar:

You: What's wrong?
Her: Nothing.
You: Nothing? Come on, what's wrong?
Her: Nothing.
You: Well, *something's* wrong. What is it?
Her: I said, "Nothing!"
You: Okay, okay. Nothing.

You get the idea here: This goes on for hours. It's happened to you, yes? Finally:

You: Please, *please.* Just tell me what's wrong.
Her: You . . . you just never *talk* to me.

When this happens, as it must, don't lose your temper. Women, too, have the right to *not* explain.

KEEPING EVERYTHING RUNNING SMOOTHLY

Are we not men? Do we not have an instinctive understanding of the physics of machinery? Can we not, given sufficient time, figure out how almost anything works?

As it is with chain saws and toaster ovens, so it is with cohabitation.

Look at the Parts. Let's see, there's you. And there's her. And there's a shared dwelling. Three parts, only two of them movable. In theory, a live-in relationship should be a masterpiece of modern technology.

But no. First off, there's a whole world of *maintenance*. Remember how well the machine ran when it was new? One reason for that was proper lubrication. And almost anybody can tell you that *courtliness* and *salaciousness* are the civilizing ointments a live-in romance needs. Did you buy her flowers before she moved in? Then you can't let up. When you dated her, did you stand up like a gentleman when she approached the table? Then on your feet, buster. If you courted her before you won her, *you must continue to court her after you've won her.* She is, after all, your girlfriend, even if you marry her and even if she hangs around for a lifetime. And good manners are as important in private as they are in public.

Now for the salaciousness part:

Sex. Don't leave all the responsibilities of romance to her. You owe it to yourself and to your lover to try to make some sexual encounters more electric than others. Make it a point to talk about sex every now and then, or to create expectations and allow for a little drama. Above all, avoid self-consciousness; spontaneity and seduction are difficult things to pull off after a couple has been living together for a time, and boredom in a sexual relationship is a terminal illness.

Conversation provides the locomotive power for most relationships. It must be assumed that you had something in common before you started sharing the TV. So talk to her. Better yet, listen to her.

But remember: This is your home, not the set of "Sally Jessy Raphael." You don't have to spill your guts all over the kitchen floor every night after work. Talk about sex and Russians and tax shelters, but try not to embarrass yourself. Of course, everybody likes a little reassurance now and then, but don't make your girlfriend do heavy lifting by trying to boost your sagging self-esteem. Remember, she's your lover, not your shrink.

OCCAM'S SUICIDE RAZOR

Bad emotions drive out worthy ones.

Jealousy is a decent emotion, the industrial average of a relationship, and a reliable sort of barometer of romantic investment. Kept in perspective, it both reassures and comforts. Nurture it, though, and it grows like a radioactive rodent and eats you alive in the night. If groundless jealousy has gotten the best of you, there's something else wrong—likely some weirdness you're cultivating—and you're ignoring it. If you have grounds for jealousy, then you have grounds for a confrontation.

Anger is our friend. Shake hands with your temper and get to know it well enough that you can control it if you quarrel with that damned annoying sweetheart of yours. Letting off a little steam isn't always a bad thing, but if the only way you can manifest anger is physically, then get help.

Depression. Every now and then, either you or your girlfriend will wake up to the existential cancer that gnaws at all of us. You'll become sullen and sore and really unpleasant company. When a woman does this, you'll feel somehow responsible. You're not, probably. Try to avoid the typical manly response to these kinds of complaints—that they are part of something you have to fix. You can't make someone else permanently happy. Period.

So if the light of your life has been dimmed by the big rheostat of existence, let her solve her own problem. The best way to deal with the happiness of your partner is to offer a good ear and almost no advice.

Or to get out of the way. Either way, don't volunteer to take it personally. Martyrdom is for moms.

RULES OF COMBAT

Some simple battle plans:

• **Don't go blindly into battle.** Fighting, after all, is not worthwhile unless you are clear about what you wish to gain.

• When you fight with the woman you love, **cloak yourself in dignity, reason, and a sense of justice.** Don't raise your voice except to steer the argument in a reasonable direction. State as often as necessary the issue being argued; make sure you're fighting about the right thing, and not about some hidden misdemeanor. Men do pretty well at logic, while women do better at intuition. Therefore, when you fight, your job is to not only argue your case, but also, in a way, to help her argue hers. Listen to what she has to say. One couple—Washingtonians—spent eighteen months yelling at each other on the phone, trying to get past their anger so they could settle up in divorce court without having to go to bankruptcy court, too. The guy finally got the temperature down by offering her a statement of her complaints, and by the time they had finally calmed down enough to get things straight for a divorce-court judge, they had talked their way back into their marriage.

• But **don't bother refuting every point.** Good fights have a symphonic effect, and it's the feeling, the overarching *mood*—the rhapsodic residue, if you will—of the thing that matters most in the end. You will have conclusively proved all the important points of any given argument, only to find that, somehow, she won—just because it *feels* like you lost. Trust your feelings on this one: If it feels like you lost, you lost.

• **Turn the fight into a conversation** at the first opportunity, then guide it to a resolution that will involve a mutual compromise. Hence:

• **Don't argue to win.** Most relationships have very few nonnegotiable points—having children, maybe, and probably fidelity. After that, who cares, really? Give in whenever you feel you have proved to yourself that your point of view is just and right. That is, argue only up to the point that you have earned the right to say you told her so when the inevitable truth of your position is finally finessed into the open by circumstances. In fact, assuming you're not arguing over some Big Question, the only reason *not* to surrender is if you think doing so will endanger your children, relationship, or job.

• ***Don't hit.*** Ever. No matter what. Everything you've ever heard since you were two years old about not hitting girls is true.

AN ESSENTIAL DIGRESSION ON THE SUBJECT OF VIOLENCE

Violence is a popular item in our culture, and it comes in unisex styles and sizes. Virtually every romantic comedy has a literal punch line that usually involves a woman hitting a man square in the nose and knocking him into a cake or under a locomotive. We all know that in domestic disputes, almost any man would gladly accept getting hit up alongside the head with a board in exchange for the sort of emotional pain that it seems only the woman he loves has the power to inflict. But try to bear in mind that while emotional violence may break a heart, physical violence can end a life.

Generally, where there's hostility in a home, it's a pervasive thing, part of a secret, domestic language, and in that climate of violence, women sometimes harm children and clobber men physically and emotionally. While we can easily get help to protect the kids, most of us feel—perhaps wrongly—that there's not much we can do about an abusive wife or girlfriend, other than look for the door, and maybe that's true.

But we *can* do something about violence against women and children by men. This sort of abuse is happening more and more; if there really is any movement in the so-called Men's Movement, maybe Robert Bly and his big guys ought to focus a little more on how many men seem to find it just as easy to beat a kid as a tom-tom, and a little less on pampering their own precious inner children.

There is no justification for a man hitting a woman or a child. When a man beats a woman or a child, he discards whatever masculine virtues he may have once possessed, and no great job, no fast car, no public acclaim, no whining apology can ever make him whole again, for he lost his manhood when he lost his reason. A man who hits women or children must be healed by a different sort of restorative. One of the very few real, nontransferable roles we have in society calls for us to protect women and children at all costs, even from ourselves. If you hit, get help—and stay away until you do.

SEX

Fighting is often what you do if you're too tired for sex. Do not confuse the two. They only look and sound the same.

Frequency. Sex has long been a source of fascination for statisticians, many of whom may have a limited sex life anyway. But the numerical value of sexual *frequency* has a quality that fascinates and beguiles us all, since it tells us not only how we're doing, but also how Mr. and Mrs. Jones next door are doing.

Once, Dan Rather was beat up on the street by two mysterious strangers who kept asking him, "What's the frequency, Kenneth? What's the frequency?" Rather was unable to come up the correct answer: 2.4 times per week on average. But don't keep track, and don't worry about it. You'll know *instantly* if your frequency should be adjusted lower, or if you should be aiming for something truly supersonic.

PRIVACY

Line of Sight. If you want to be happy for the rest of your life, never make an ugly woman your wife. There's nothing wrong with a little scenery around the house.

But watch out for too much of a good thing. You're in for big trouble if you find you have to keep your eye on your sweetie simply because there's no place else to look. *Never try to live with someone else in a house or apartment where there's no place to hide.* Insist on your privacy when you need it, and don't intrude on hers, either.

Bathroom Etiquette. Don't try to become as one in the bathroom. One at a time, please. Don't allow her to shit while you shave.

Separate but Equal. Look, if somebody told you that he liked to grease up with baby oil and crawl around barking like a doggy while his wife shouted at him in German, you'd shrug your shoulders and say, "Whatever." Right? Well, imagine the shock if your pal told you he and his wife slept in separate bedrooms. You'd think the guy was odd, a weirdo, a freak, a pervert. You never know what works. If a little privacy makes life with your wife more intriguing, add on a room.

Your Body, Your Own Self. Incidentally, if you're just going through the initial, traumatic phase of trying to live a normal life with another person's body walking around your house and your sex drive has flagged—even after a monumental splurge of seed-distribution—don't worry. The last resort for those craving their old sense of privacy is to withdraw physically. One guy stopped sleeping with his girlfriend two weeks after she moved in and didn't sleep with her again until she threatened to leave. Some guys just run for cover. Don't make it into a big problem—but don't make it a habit, either.

HOUSEWORK

Careful here. Part of the deal with which you were seduced involved all that domestic bliss action, remember? All those wonderful visions of hot dinners served on a clean TV tray?

Born to Be a Bachelor. If it turns out that the price you pay for that is heavy housework, make your bargain with clear vision. If part of your domestic routine involved clean kitchens and the like *before* she moved in, then you're honor-bound to do your part thereafter. But if you were always a sloppy bachelor and you liked being a sloppy bachelor, then you have the right to change the bachelor part without disturbing the sloppy part. For example, if clean dishes were always a part of your evening program, then get in there and roll up your sleeves. But if you were always content letting your dirty dishes support another, more hideous part of the food chain, then don't turn over a clean plate just for her.

The limit here, of course, is one of consideration: If you were a congenital swine, don't take advantage of your birthright. Common rooms, especially, need not be vulgar rooms.

A Useful but Complicated Justification for Benign Sloth. There's more to this insistent demand for cleanliness on the part of women than meets the eye, needless to say. To get to the meaning of cleaning, you have to step back a pace or two and take a long look at the big picture.

To start with, the clean-people have a firm grip on the moral edge: *Civilized men may not argue against cleanliness.* Besides, cleaning, as a lifestyle choice, has more than a fair amount of positive spin to it: There's nothing like the idea of a brisk cleaning to sort of make you feel reborn, cleaners say. A clean slate, and all that. But invariably a taste of cleanliness leads to filthy excess. Let's say, for example, you're a middle-aged guy working for Acme, Inc., maybe in sales, maybe in shipping, doesn't matter, you get the idea: Same place every day, same lousy boss, same wife, same kids, same everything. One day you wake up, see that most of your life is covered with dust, that there are cobwebs hanging off your loftiest ambitions, so, quite reasonably, you say to yourself, "Whoa, let's get rid of some of this stuff." So you divorce your wife, abandon your children, and make off to Florida with this manicurist you met who can really read the road map of your soul. That's a spring clean. But, oh dear, what a mess.

It's not always one's personal life that gets rubbed out by the impulse to scour. An illustration of overclean: Once, a certain Modern Man listened while his neighbor talked about an old house he owned on a shady lot in an obscure corner of Pennsylvania. The house had been deserted for years, but it was still a charming building, full of possibilities. When the Modern Man next saw his neighbor standing in front of the house with a full contingent of cousins and kids, he asked him what he had in mind. "Not much," the man said. "I'm just going to clean up a little."

Dangerous talk. Sure enough, within two weeks he had dismantled the place and burned what was left. There was nothing left. *Nothing.* The lot was as empty as Sinead O'Connor's fuzzy little noggin. A day or two later, the Modern Man collared his neighbor at the local IGA. "I thought you were just going to clean up that old house."

He looked at our man as if he were nuts and said, "I did."

Two days later, somebody pulled a mobile home onto the lot, plugged her in, and turned on the TV.

The My Lai Stratagem. The lesson? Sometimes, you've got to destroy the place in order to clean it up.

There is a Serbian variation on this theme, the dark side of regional maintenance, in which whole precincts are leveled in order to "cleanse" them, ethnically speaking, since the Serbs apparently feel their enemies are too dirty to live next door. Profoundly hygienic feminists, allied with a whole legion of right-wing religious nuts, feel likewise about cootie-laden depictions of sex and so want to disinfect the film, book, and magazine industries. In cities and towns everywhere, anxious parents, alarmed by contaminated books like *Huckleberry Finn* and *The Catcher in the Rye,* want to clean up America's public library shelves. Urban planners want to clean up inner cities by building newer ghettos. Green is clean, even though Nature isn't. In fact, the whole history of twentieth-century progressivism in America has been one big Pine Sol party: Give a smug, middle-class white liberal too much free time and a bucketful of rectitude, and he'll want to clean up everybody's act.

So don't get soap in your eyes as you slip down the well-scrubbed road to hell; don't lose your soul in the lather of good intentions. The next time you get told to clean the attic, ask her what she has against the First

Amendment. Women want to know why men don't do their fair share around the house? We do—by drawing a line in the dirt and grease and saying, in one way or another, "Beyond this point, all is to no avail." Some things in life just won't come clean, and some things in life ought not be cleaned at all. Mostly, though, lots of things in life just aren't that dirty.

The Exception. The trash. Men were born to take out the trash. Figuratively, literally.

TIME TO MOVE ON

When you live with a woman, you are on a date that has no kiss good night, no clammy front-door handshake. But it's only a date. There are always other options, other places to live, other people to live with. When it's time to move on, the exit signs are obvious: You resent her presence and look forward to her absences and abhor the sound of her voice and marvel that she ever looked good enough to make you make a fool of yourself.

On the other hand, if you've been judicious in your choice of live-in lover, you just might want to alter the relationship slightly. In fact, you just might want to marry her. (Commit to memory all you have read in this and the previous chapters, then, quick, turn the page.)

CHAPTER FIVE

MODERN MARRIAGE

Every now and then, love just gets so crazy it has to be institutionalized.

Marriage—that nutty dream of every mad lover from John Alden to John Hinckley—is the Swiss Army knife of social conventions, one shiny package jammed full of surprising and useful features. It has, for instance, always been the therapeutic tool we use to calm one of our most irrational passions: If nothing else, marriage gets the mad dog of lust off the streets for a time and makes the world a little safer for our daughters. It provides respectability to many who could never hope to be respectable in any other pursuit, and it creates jobs for marriage counselors and others who would never otherwise find employment. For many, marriage provides a swell sort of emotional BarcaLounger, something remarkably comfortable, if somewhat unfashionable, to fall back on. For all of us, it's the next thing you do after the last date you have.

The essential benefits of marriage, especially monogamous marriage, are twofold. First, it keeps us from confusing sex-without-guilt with sex-without-responsibility. Second, it protects children and women—a notion that appeals to men's better selves. So marriage, for most of us, is a good idea.

When it's not a good idea, you find out right away.

THE TECHNOLOGICAL OBSOLESCENCE OF WOMEN

After two centuries of ostentatious Puritanism, the sudden emergence in this country of nudity on TV might have carried with it the seed of a tremendous social revolution, for what with microwave ovens in the kitchen *and* naked ladies on TV, it might be argued that men really don't need live-in women at all anymore. Maybe all a fellow really has to do is put a blonde fright wig on the microwave and marry it, then go off and have an affair with the VCR. If our man wants a touchy-feely, intimate, get-to-know-me-and-my-feelings-about-my-Dad conversation, he can dial a 900 number.

Live wives? Ha! This is the dawn of the twenty-first century, pal. You got your pick of a hundred, no, a *thousand* beautiful women. You can drop off Friday's bride where you got her and marry three buxom Brazilian bimbos the next day. You can pack a studio apartment with a whole screaming seraglio of slo-mo starlets and give 'em all the slip if you want a beer with the guys at the corner pump. If they complain, you can turn 'em off as quickly as you turned 'em on. Or turn 'em in for somebody new and more understanding and more blonde. Thanks to mostly American technology, for the first time in a million generations *you can live like a man*—you can eat pizza for breakfast, smoke cigars in the bathtub, swing from the doorjambs, and talk to yourself in guttural, simianlike grunts. You can leave the toilet seat up forever in a permanent salute to the good old stand-up leakeroo, the kind that leaves the john looking like a big, steaming bowl of heady piss beer.

The Safest Sex. And, believe it or not, this is really happening. Apparently, some guys are willing to deal with a string of troubled and troublesome women only up to a certain point in their lives, and once they reach that point, the women on video are far more inviting than the ones that scream into the phone. One man, a successful professional living in California who had had a long and enjoyable bachelor existence in dateland, finally gave up when he couldn't find a reasonable woman who could sustain a relationship for more than a few months and when he felt the threat of AIDS closed down the possibility of easily finding somebody new. For the past five years, he has essentially taken his sex life into his own hands, if you get the drift, and most of his hot dates these days are with rented videotapes. His suggestions? "Make a night of it—shower, shave, just like you were going to go out." You can get dressed or not, look great or not, pour yourself a drink and relax. He says he's been seeing the same video store rental inventory for three years and is happy at last. "I don't miss women. They're still around. I see them, sometimes I even date them. I just don't get involved with them."

There. So, strictly speaking, we can leave the woman thing behind us. Yet for most of us it just hasn't happened. Call it a traditional, pre-tech affection if you want to, but apparently most men have convinced themselves that they can't live without women any more than they can live without TV.

WHAT TO LOOK FOR IN YOUR BASIC WIFE

Men (and women, for that matter) spend most of their first two or three decades like teens in a premarital mall, just hanging out, window-shopping, occasionally slipping something on, but not really buying. It's a shopping experience we have all shared. If you were one of the ones who left the mall married, then you know that what happened was psychedelic, man: Suddenly one day you started hallucinating signs that read FINAL DAYS! CLEARANCE SALE! and you grabbed something—anything—on the way out.

There are only a half-dozen things to consider when you decide to take a wife. Six. That's not many. But skip just one, and you'll be doomed to repeat the other five.

1. *Marry the most beautiful woman you can find.* Writer-producer Bruce Henstell once pointed out that every woman has one good picture, one shot from one angle that makes her look just wonderful. It's the shot you see when you first fall in love with a woman, and from that moment on, it's the only picture of her that exists for you.

Women are far more realistic in these matters, and once they leave adolescence, they look for qualities in a man that often have little to do with his appearance, thank God. But we're hounds, every one of us, and for us, it's packaging that makes the sale—and keeps us away from the return counter. If a woman has a dazzling personality or a spirituality that blinds you to her appearance, don't worry: You'll patch something together in your imagination that will keep her looking beautiful forever.

Meanwhile, don't get hoodwinked by movie-perfect women. We're a species obsessed with images of beauty. We worship beauty and often feel less than beautiful ourselves. So while we make women who happen to conform to the prevailing standard of beauty abstract objects of desire, we also alienate them, make them into people unlike the rest of us. Since everybody does this to beautiful women, a beautiful woman can be isolated by her appearance and hence desperately lonely for a little civil company. The trite tip-off to an ugly blind date is the promise that she has a great personality, since we don't normally associate great personalities with pretty women (and men especially don't describe a woman in terms of her character unless there's *nothing* good to say about the way she looks). For many beautiful women, appearance becomes a genuine burden, what with a world of men looking for just the right accent piece to set off the beach house or the Porsche.

On the other hand, attractive women who use their good looks as a replacement part for other important character qualities, like wit or kindness or competence, make expensive but very convenient Bic wives. They're disposable, but at least they know it. Like ball players, they have to get it while they can, because when the fat lady sings, it's all over, especially if they've become the fat lady.

2. *Marry for laughs.* Dull and stupid women, self-serious women, and boring women all have no sense of humor, the one unfailing measure of intelligence. Find somebody who knows a joke when she tells it.

3. *Marry a grown-up woman.* Who said kids grow up too fast? While it's true that many men die of old age while in the throes of a mid-adolescent crisis, lots of girls will be girls until they finally decide to be postmenopausal women. For some girls—and this applies especially to white girls—postcollegiate life in the big city is just paid graduate work. Their lives take on the familiar simplicity of campus dwellers:

- *The serious ones* join the urban-professional equivalent of a sorority, they run the school newspaper and work on the campus radio station, they organize pep rallies and marches, they just adore popular profs, and they get real mad at the dean. They form odd cliques, travel in groups, go nuts for fads, and play follow-the-leader.
- *The not-so-serious ones* cultivate their social standing in the cafeteria, go to lots of dances, and still see drugs as a metaphor for the smartness of youth.

They all mistake this extended adolescence for adulthood. Alas, they are often unhappy, and their unhappiness ultimately becomes an issue that they explore in focus groups and seminar-type settings, until they finally have an epiphany: They decide the problem is you.

Unless you too are involved in putting together a back-to-school lifestyle, marrying an adolescent woman is a sure disaster, since she'll never grow up enough to have real-life competence.

4. *Marry for sex.* Married life is rough; sex is the lubricant and leveler. Besides, sex is one of the very few human activities shared by both genders that, in practice, has no rhetorical value.

5. *Marry for money.* No, no, not *her* money, knucklehead. *Yours.* A chap knows he's made a good marriage when he sees how much better he's doing as a consequence of marrying a smart woman than he was as a wasted bachelor. In their spare time, and without even breaking a sweat, good wives help build great careers for their husbands, for women are practical, and, as well-noted, wives are practical about husbands.

You can, of course, marry for *her* money, but trust us on this one: You'll earn every penny. Plus, you'll have lousy job security.

6. *Marry for kids.* This is short, so read it twice. There are many women who do not wish to be involved mothers, who feel life without kids is plenty interesting enough, and who find such satisfaction in other endeavors that they don't need whatever it is motherhood has to offer. *These women make great dates.* But you don't have to marry any of them, especially if at some time in your life you want to be somebody's dad. A good father will *only* marry a woman who wants to be a good mother.

ACCESSORIES AND OPTIONS

Let's see what sort of mileage we can get out of this Trabant-like, women-as-cars metaphor. While some women care not to be discussed in other than literal terms, men live in a parallel universe filled with analogies that rattle around like loose lug nuts in a cheap, Korean hubcap. For example: If you want a wife that's fully loaded, look for these little extras:

• In terms of design, *get something functional,* but avoid wagons and vans.

• *You'll eventually outgrow a convertible,* and, besides, they provide almost no creature comforts.

• *Coupes are a better bet,* since a lithe, sleek look always suggests a sporty attitude, especially if you avoid the current affection for puffy, rounded edges. And while they aren't spacious, a coupe is usually sufficient to accommodate two small backseat passengers.

• *Upholstery* can be seductive. Rich, plush appointments often seem like a good idea at the time, but if your interests are appropriately superficial, go for vinyl and forget the velour. Vinyl never ages. Look at Cher.

• *A/C, P/S, P/B, A/T, cruise.* Cool is good, of course. The other amenities make life on the road safer, easier, less tiresome, easier to handle. Good maintenance is essential, however.

• *Get something with power.* Every now and then, you just want to get out there on the four-lane, blow out the carbon, and remember what it was like the first time you did this.

• *Visit the factory.* Check out Mom and Dad. Any important body parts missing—like brains, for instance? Her parents' home is the house that will haunt her forever, so give it a close once-over, since you'll soon be living in the figurative attic.

BUREAU OF MARITAL CONTRACTS, DEPARTMENT OF BLISS

Varieties of Religious Experience. There are two fundamentally different ways to look at a wedding. To some, it's a church thing. To others, it's a state affair.

For the religious, a marriage ceremony only incidentally involves a civil contract. Mostly, it is a sacrament in which a vow is made in the presence of God and man.

For many others, however, a wedding is the beginning of the secular life we live with women, and hence falls at least partially under the purview of this work.

So Choose. A religious ceremony or a civil one? It's a mistake to confuse these two types of weddings, by the way. If you have even the slightest doubt that your marriage will survive every single one of life's obstacles, then don't take marriage vows in a church or synagogue, despite the fact that these buildings provide a nice, traditional backdrop. Get married at City Hall or stand up in front of a clerk at Sea World or go someplace else, because on the off-chance that there's something to this whole God question—and on the even more remote possibility that churches have something to do with it—it's a much smarter gambit to tell a lie to a bureaucrat than a clergyman.

Smartest of all is to skip the wedding part completely if you have even the slightest doubt about the ultimate success of the gambit. But don't worry: Everybody has doubts, yet nobody takes this kind of advice. Most people go to their weddings filled with equal parts hope and dread, and they figure the rest out later.

Formal Weddings. Discussing marriage ceremonies in conceptual terms is one thing, but there's no sense in going into the phenomenal flatulence and vulgarity that defines formal modern weddings. Once you decide to get married, it's all out of your hands anyway. While your bride and her family will be doing the important work of the ceremony and reception—hiring the caterer, finding a band, refinancing their house— you only have to remember three relatively minor things:

- Show up.
- Don't get in the way.
- Don't fall over.

Civil Ceremonies. These have the advantage of being unpretentious by definition: The ritual of the bureaucrat is a stark and practical thing, concerned mostly with getting the forms completed and collecting the fees.

Gas-Man Weddings. Someday, when the world is a smarter place, we'll have the utility company's meter reader do weddings. You'll call and ask for a wedding at 241 Nadir Circle. The guy will show up at breakfast, read the meter, get you and the Mrs. to shake hands, and have you sign form 241, a marriage certificate. He'll say, "Congrats, see ya." A month later, a $15 surcharge will show up on your bill. Quiet, discreet, personal—just the way an exchange of intimate promises ought to be. Not only that, but you'll have thirty days to decide whether or not you were just kidding.

HOW YOU GET MARRIED

There is, ever so obviously, a profound distinction between getting married and going to a wedding. If you can read a map, you can get to the wedding. It's how you ended up married that's hard to figure.

It's causality that confuses us. From adolescence we have practiced the liturgy of lust, from a kiss to a feel to a thigh to a touchdown. But we never quite saw where that was all leading, until we found ourselves standing there promising away half our worldly goods.

Unhappily, we just can't see very far. As we've seen, usually it works like this: A man meets a woman, and, based almost solely on her appearance (augmented sometimes by a decent personality or other marginal factors, like intelligence), he pursues her. His objective is usually quite limited. Maybe he just wants to see if she's a pleasant dinner companion, or maybe he's after uncomplicated sex. In any case, he doesn't see where a simple introduction might lead until he's finally at a point where *he realizes he can do nothing other than marry her.*

But of course a courtship, however brief, is a collection of such moments. We may call them dates, if we wish. These encounters are trees; the relationship is the forest. Viewed in the hot Aristotelian light men prefer, trees are all we can see. We know when we pick her up that the episode at hand will have a beginning, a middle, and an end. We've planned the beginning and the middle; it's the end that holds us in thrall. We have to see what's going to happen, so our sight is fixed on reaching the finale—the handshake, the shrug, the slap of sweaty bellies, whatever happens to tell us that the encounter is over. Men sense the pleasure of this sort of balance, and they cannot shake this quest for *telos;* we are made uncomfortable by engaging in any task without a full understanding of its end, its meaning, its goal. If women shared this dubious quality, they would understand why we *must* go to sleep immediately after sex. We just like to finish what we start.

A typical woman sees things much more clearly than does a typical man. Rather than looking at a relationship as a series of structured encounters, she sees it as an elaborate syllogism, in which certain hypotheses are proved by that which has preceded them. In English: While each date has for her a certain kind of free-form, improvisational quality, she sees that if a courtship is proceeding down a figurative aisle, each one of these encounters will lead to another, different, more complex encounter, until finally you are brought to the last date. In handyman's terms: She asks you to make a series of objects—a bookshelf, a planter shaped like a goose, a wooden table. Then one day she tells you that you've built a house, and asks you to please shut the door because there's a draft.

SOMETIMES, A WOMAN'S GOTTA DO . . .

Marriage Is to Women What Work Is to Men. For men, work—a job, a career, the paycheck concept thing—is an elaborate fiction designed to minimalize meaninglessness in life and maximize rewards. Women see marriage (and a consequent family) the same way. The difference: Work really *is* meaningless. Class? Compare and contrast (a) women who put career ahead of family with (b) men who put family ahead of career.

LOSER TOONS

Fifty years ago, if you became conversationally loose with a woman, she'd tell you about all the terrific suitors she had had and how she had dismissed them all with broken hearts. Today, as you already know if you're on friendly terms with almost any single woman, she'll tell you about all the many, many suitors she's had who were not so terrific. Virtually every unmarried woman over the age of, say, twenty-five or thirty has a jam-packed gallery of rogue males who have trampled on her hopes and dreams: men who were married, men who drank, men who were closet hermits, men who killed their cats, men who wore her skirts. Unsuitable men. "Men are such jerks," she'll say at some point.

It's Her Problem. Most women crave justification for ill-advised behavior, and those who choose (and frequently marry) a long sequence of lunatics and philanderers are on the run from responsibility and just don't want to feel bad about it. If you're a lunatic or a philanderer, you may wish to help them. If not, remember: Most women spend at least part of their postadolescence in this sort of state, and if you happen along during this stage of her life and are looking for any reasonable long-term relationship, she'll boot you out of there, pronto. If a complicated relationship is what she'd wanted, she'd have it.

Time's Up. Most women decide on a mature marriage at a certain point—often in their late twenties or early thirties—and, armed with a new, crisp realism, they marry the first eligible chap to come along after that decision has been made. Usually, this decision is made with what to us, with our pull-down-our-pants-style of cogitation, must seem an almost coldhearted deliberation. Smart women—the sort of women *you* want to marry—simply and wisely wish to be convinced of the aptness of their men, and they make their choices almost without regard to whatever transpired in their premarital lives. Suddenly, all those charming nights with motorcycle gangs and guys with red rubber noses and water balloons are things of the past. For women, there's a big difference between getting down and getting down to business.

WHY WOMEN MARRY

As H. L. Mencken points out in his *In Defense of Women,* you may think you're a prize, but to your wife, you're second-rate at best.

Women Begin Their Love Life Lost in Fantasy. According to Mencken, women make their first choice in a man while still quite young, and the object of their heart may not even be a real person: He may be a character in a movie or book. Or he might be a very distant ideal, maybe a singer or a TV personality. Probably, he's not a politician.

From that point onward, it's just one abrasive compromise after another, until she settles for you—perhaps her fiftieth choice.

She Never Forgets One Through Forty-Nine. In fact, no one is more aware of her husband's shortcomings than his wife. Not only is he a disappointment in comparison with all those idealized men who for years have paraded through her imagination—or, maybe, her bedroom—but he reinforces her notions of his own dorkishness by gaining in incompetence what he has lost in independence.

Still, you must have had something going for you, once—even if only momentarily and when very drunk. When she finally settled for you, she formulated a number of reasonable considerations:

• *Security.* A woman may want to mother your children, but she may not wish to mother you—especially if you seem bent on stretching your teenage years well into your forties as you pursue some juvenile, self-inflated image of the person you'd be if only life would hand you a break.

One fellow, an Iowan, claims to be charming, witty, intelligent, and, as he puts it, "cute," whatever that means. He is also chronically unemployable, with a massive chip on his shoulder as a consequence, and is determined to marry a rich woman. He can't figure out why women dump him as soon as he gets serious about marriage, but he thinks it might be because he hasn't made more than $7,500 in any of the last ten years.

He's quite right. Men like this exist to provide premarital women with an entertaining social life. When women get serious about marriage, they get serious men, since most women prefer not to help men find themselves, and most women prefer men who are able to do a man's work—namely, support himself and his family. *This is true even if she already has a career;* in fact, a woman who already deals with workaday responsibilities is even more clear in her expectations, and she will have a well-informed appreciation of what it will take to get by if she decides to opt for full-time motherhood.

• **Dad.** According to a legion of shrinks, women marry as part of a reaction against their fathers. *This is psychology,* so it may be more a feeling than a truth.

• **Mom.** Same source: Some women get married in order to become their mothers. Some men love to be mothered. These two types get together and you have all the magic and excitement of higher mathematics, but with none of the resolution.

• **Respect.** Never underestimate the importance of a woman's self-esteem—and the esteem of her friends and family—in making her choice. The best women marry men whose qualities match their own healthy self-esteem. On the other hand, insecure men frequently marry trophy wives—especially if their insecurity is caused by advancing age. So do women wed trophy husbands, but women are considerably more adroit in masquerading their motives for marriage.

• **Children.** Most women earnestly desire to have children and, in cooperation with a responsible, sensible father (and, really, many desperate women even skip the sensible part), to be good mothers to the children they have.

SMART BUT DEAD MEN SPOUT OFF ON MARRIAGE

Thinking about marriage, eh? You're not the first guy:

• *". . . to avoid fornication, let every man have his own wife, and let every woman have her own husband."*

—*St. Paul*

• *"Have you not heard*
   When a man marries, dies, or turns Hindoo,
   His best friends hear no more of him?"

—*Percy Bysshe Shelley*

•*"Marriage . . . combines the maximum of temptation with the maximum of opportunity."*

—George Bernard Shaw

•*"The reasons why so few marriages are happy is because young ladies spend their time in making nets, not in making cages."*

—Jonathan Swift

•*"Many a man in love with a dimple makes the mistake of marrying the whole girl."*

—Stephen Leacock

• *"Romances paint at full length people's wooings,*
  But only give a bust of marriages:
For no one cares for matrimonial cooings,
  There's nothing wrong in a connubial kiss:
Think you, if Laura had been Petrarch's wife,
He would have written sonnets all his life?"

—George Gordon, Lord Byron

DEATH, TAXES, AND THE LAWS OF MARRIAGE

Some things you can't help but notice:

• **Lafavore's Law of Incipient Idiocy.** Marriage makes you stupid. Explanation: Under the constant scrutiny of their wives, who are always wondering why they made the choice they did, men begin to glow with perspiration, because inevitably the result of this ongoing surveillance is an increasingly acute sensitivity to our manifold inadequacies. Worried about meeting not only our responsibilities, but also our wives' expectations, and aware of every minor failure, no matter how insignificant, we begin to fear we are slowly becoming the idiots our wives already suspected we were anyway.

• *The Brooks Corollary.* Your wife will pick a fight with you when you look your stupidest—i.e., half-shaved, in boxers, or while flossing.

• *Smith's Rule of Conversational Constipation.* Your wife will invariably launch into a lengthy discourse at the exact moment you seek to excuse yourself to attend the toilet.

There are many corollaries to Smith's Rule, most notably:

• *The MacNeil-Lehrer Corollary.* During the evening newscast, your wife will remain silent during commercials and talk through the news. Some wives, by the way, believe they are performing this as a service to their husbands and see their running commentaries on the news as a sort of closed-captioning device for the thinking-impaired.

• *The Lawrence Corollary.* The longer you wait to catch a baseball score, the more likely it is that your wife will ask you an idle question at the exact moment the score is reported.

• There is also at least one distaff application, to wit, *The Lomas Rule of Methane Prophylaxis.* Your wife will break wind within five seconds of your decision to initiate romance.

• *The Menninger Maneuver.* The later it is, the more tired you are, the more important the breakfast meeting the next morning, the more likely your wife is to attempt to seduce you.

• *The Swinburnian Restatement.* A wife gives a glance when she knows there's no chance.

• *Stan's Rule of Three.* The statute of limitations for misdemeanors committed in the heart—glancing at other women, for instance, or remarking on another woman's remarkableness—is either three days or three years. If your wife is still talking about your transgression after three days, she'll remember it for three years.

• *Ranson's Actuarial Observation.* A marriage that lasts eight years will last a lifetime.

It should be noted that this hopeful marital law is widely reported using different numbers, ranging from three to fifteen. Lois Ranson claims to have her number on authority of her own statistical analysis.

• *Willis's Law of Woman-Flushing.* You meet more attractive, available women during the first year of your marriage than you did in all the years preceding your marriage.

MAKING HAY

Scrape off them shoes, sit a spell, and let's talk hay with a Modern Man from southern Nebraska.

If you bale hay while it's still too green, and then stack it compactly in a wooden barn, you'll get a dramatic demonstration of spontaneous combustion. All that pressure, all that heat from all that rot. Within minutes, you'll have no hay, no barn, no nothin'.

• *Cut your field high* enough to allow the hay to settle on a couple of inches of stubble.

• *Let the air circulate* under it while it cures. Turn it once if you have to.

• *Make sure your rows are spread evenly.* Don't allow green hay to pile up in tight patches of low-lying thatch, where decay can set in.

• *When you put it up,* make sure it's in a dry mow in a well-maintained barn. A little salt will help draw out extra moisture. Well-cured hay eventually will mold badly and deteriorate if you let the rain get to it.

If you take care, your hay will keep its nutrient value longer, other farmers will envy your neat and tidy haystack, and you'll never run the risk of an unexpected flare-up.

Smart guys make marriages the same way they make hay.

MARITAL MOJO

The Quest for Postmarital Sex. You meet a woman and fall in love and she's not safe with you in the same room. You can't keep your hands off her, you devise Oriental positions and play out fantasies with her like the despicable pervert you have become. You swive and rut and when she's not around, you're a one-armed fool with nothing but her on your mind. You're a monogamous sex fiend.

Then you get married, and you start to lose things. Like your sex drive. Where the hell did that thing go? you wonder. It was here just a second ago. . . .

• *Don't look for what isn't missing.* Don't mistake passion's pubescent fervor for sex. Sex is like soybeans. It's the miracle filler found in almost every aspect of married life. You can hide it under a layer of affectionate sentimentality or serve it up naked as passion.

• *Passion isn't the normal symptom of sex.* The sexual marathon that often precedes infatuation's grand finale is not a static condition of life with women. If it were, nobody'd be able to work. Or walk. So long as there is a sexual context to your marriage—that is, so long as you see your marital partner as a sexual being at least part of the time—then passion will take care of itself. Remember how, in the throes of lust, it seemed like your dick lived a secret life all its own? So does passion. Passion keeps its own calendar and comes out to celebrate its own private holidays. You'll be the first to know.

• *Make room for sex.* Nothing fills up a house like a marriage. Two people can live together in relative sexual bliss for years. You add a marriage contract and suddenly there's no room for *anything*. The place is packed; you can't turn around.

Clear away a little extra space for some sex—some evening during prime time, or some afternoon instead of work. By the way, if you think it's crowded with two married people in one house, remember this: Children are on constant guard against sex; if the Border Patrol did for the borders what kids do for sex, the only illegal aliens in America would be from Mars.

• *Think dirty thoughts.* Don't let your love object cease to be a sex object. Experiment. Watch an erotic film, invite the Sharon Stone of your mind to join you for a little threesome, sit around naked with antlers on your head, or talk to each other like cheap, carny trash. Between married couples, anything goes that works.

• *Remain on intimate terms.* The relationship you enjoy with your wife should always be an intimate one. The best way to do this: Allow her some privacy, maintain your own, and foster a sense of differentiation.

Another surefire way to keep a certain level of intimacy: Protect the secrets you share with your wife. Never let your sex life become the common currency of your conversation.

• *Miss her.* The only solution Mencken has to offer for this problem is to take separate vacations. If you were married to Mencken, of course, that would be perfect, but for most people it isn't a practical solution, or even a helpful one. The abstract idea is a good one, though: Too much oneness can make coupling a little problematic.

• *Don't panic.* Sometimes *sex* takes a separate vacation, and leaves one or both of you behind. If your wife suddenly seems preoccupied or otherwise distracted from sex, don't make a fuss. Marriage requires infinite flexibility. Before insisting that she always operate at your level of sexual activity, try to understand her need for a little physical withdrawal from time to time. Of course, some guys use this sort of situation as an opportunity to grab a ukulele, slip into a polyester-Hawaiian something, douse themselves with a little English Leather, and sing "My Baby Don't Give Me Good Lovin' " at the top of their lungs beneath some sympathetic single woman's window. The potted plant that inevitably clocks them on the head comes courtesy of their wives' lawyers.

• *Don't take your sexual relationship for granted.* As in other aspects of life with women, you just have to pay attention sometimes.

LOOSE SHOES

Look, no hard feelings here, but *the best women aren't terribly sentimental about this marriage business.* When a woman decides to marry, either she's been removed to a state of irrationality and will therefore marry the wrong man and so be made to suffer much distress, or she has already lived through the crazy parts of a love life and now browses for a husband with all the wild abandon of a spinster buying sensible shoes made to last. If you would have a good wife, be a wing tip, not a loafer.

Remember that, lads: A wing tip. Not a loafer.

CHAPTER SIX

MODERN MAYHEM AND CHEATING HEARTS

A guy lost in a maze comes into a room with two doors.

Not really. This is a wee morality skit, a tiny parable for a fix you've probably been in yourself once or twice, like where let's say the maze is life, the room is where you are now, and the doors are the only opportunities available to you.

So a guy lost in a maze comes to a room with two doors. He has to choose one of the two doors, but he doesn't know which. He needs a clue, so he tries to look through the keyhole of each door.

Behind one door is a well-stocked bar where a bunch of naked Swedish stewardesses are having a limbo party. He can hear music and see a few flickering neon signs in the hazy distance. The signs say, BABES! MONEY! FUN!

Behind the other is his girlfriend, his wife, the mother of his children. There's a rented video of *Pinocchio* on the box, a big pile of bills in the corner, and a dinner table on which sits meat loaf and potatoes.

- The guy can enter either door, but not both.
- Once he chooses one, he's locked in, and there's no going back.

Which door does he choose?

HOPE AND GLORY

Now, this little dilemma is only cute when you're not the guy, because for you and me and most of the guys we know, having to choose your girlfriend over a bunch of buck-naked, well-intentioned Scando tea-toters is only sometimes easy. More often, it's excruciating stuff, the kind of trial by temptation that defines what makes cheating such a transcendently fascinating concept, and such a mean, sad, and depressing deed.

The Carter Commandment: The Fruit of Deceit Smells Better Than It Tastes. There are two very popular ways to cheat. You can cheat in your heart, figuratively speaking, or you can cheat in a cheap motel, literally speaking. You get to make this choice every time Fate brings up the subject. And that, friends, is why we are here today, to consider cheating, by which we mean capital-C Cheating, as in Love Betrayal, as in Torrid Affair, as in Quick! Out the Back Door! It's My Husband! not little-c cheating, as in politics, where it's cheating not to cheat.

HOW TO CHEAT IN YOUR HEART

Conceptual Cheating. This is cheating as an art form, because there are no limits except those imposed by your own imagination. Cheating in your heart is a playground of erotic expression, where the swings and slides are found in the *potential* for dangerous pleasures and forbidden acts. If you cheat in your heart, the mere *thought* of humping hordes of reckless, Viking women (to give what for me has obviously become an increasingly compelling example) is enough to get you through many a long, long night. Indeed, simply summoning all your prodigious brain-power and cogitating with narrow focus and great ferocity on the pretty good likelihood of an evil liaison with that woman you saw give you a casual glance over the cheese in the deli section at FatMart can leave you feeling like the citizen of a planet filled with interesting possibilities. *She* *could have been yours and you know it.* Suddenly, you're a mojo-monster, a man of mighty mien and meat, a damned handsome fellow, the envy of all your pals.

There is a biblical injunction against this sort of thing, however, mostly because when the runaway sedan of imaginary seduction is careering down the winding road of fantasy, the brake pedal is damned hard to find. Especially in the dark. But a man can indulge in a little cardiac cavorting without demolishing his life or without further fraying the cheap, synthetic moral fabric of our unfortunate times, provided he maintains careful control. Besides, a little cheating in the heart can make fidelity in the bedroom a much simpler discipline.

Here is a trio o' tips for happy, heart-bound misbehavior:

• ***Shop carefully.*** Let's say Cynthia in accounting has made her unbridled desire for you quite clear. She has even said, in almost precisely these words, "You know, Bob, we need to discuss your expense account reports. Hey, I know! Let's get together some night for a drink. At my place. With no clothes on." When you go into accounting, the air around Cynthia's desk is warm with unrequited lust. You feel her eyes on you every moment. When you hand in your quarterlies, her lips part slightly and quiver almost imperceptibly. Sometimes, she looks across the office at you, pretends to stretch, puts both hands behind her neck, rolls her head back, and points her breasts at you like little, pert Scuds.

• ***Colorize it.*** Pretty soon, in the soap opera of your heart, Cynthia becomes a featured player.

What can you do to enhance this little drama? Collect data: Memorize the color of her hair, the corners of her mouth, the crook of her thumb. When you're close to Cynthia, inhale her scent until you can taste it.

But don't touch Cynthia.

Instead, borrow enough mental pieces of Cynthia that you can go home and, in the privacy of your fevered mind's basement workshop, build your own Cynthia. Then, when you hear the call of the wild salami, close your eyes. See Cynthia. See Cynthia play.

• ***Make sure you've got it right.*** Remember that in the real world, where Cynthia lives, it could be that none of this is happening. A miscalculation here—a confusion between your fantasy and Cynthia's reality—could really cost you, because Cynthia's crazy desire for you could be all *your* insanity and not Cynthia's, and if you try and make it Cynthia's, you're on the fast track to frustration and disappointment. If, for example, you boldly try to go where you were never invited in the first place, if you attempt to actually *provoke* that breast-thrusting stretch, that quivering lip, in order to achieve some Cynthiagazmic sexorama that exists *only* in your fantasy and not in reality, bingo! you're going to end up in a tangle of bad manners, humiliation, embarrassment, and, quite probably and rightly, unemployment.

THE DEED

But It Was Such a Good Idea. Yes, yes. Of course it was. Pay attention: That's what we're talking about here—cheating as a damned good idea. But before you get suckered into transforming your little idea into anything more concrete, back up a little and consider some of the little laws we live by. First, in love—and in life—remember that the latest idea isn't necessarily the best idea just because it's the latest idea. Remember? Your wife or girlfriend was also just an idea once. Now she's a better idea, even though she's not the latest idea. In fact—and second—like most ideas, the latest idea is probably a bad idea, compared to other, older, better ideas. Third, in the whole catalog of ideas, both new and old, few ideas are as bad an idea as the idea you might have about *actually* entwining Cynthia's legs with your own, live and in-concert, as it were. As an idea, great. As a deed, not great. Clear?

AN ANALOGY OVERFLOWING WITH ENVIRONMENTALLY HARMFUL METAPHORS

But let's say Cynthia's lonely, desperate . . . whatever it takes to make her wish you would make that fatal pass, forget about your wife and kids, and the devil take the hindmost—that is, when you're done with it. Really. How bad could it be?

Real bad.

See, you can cheat in your heart with Cynthia forever, until you cheat with Cynthia in her apartment. Then you can count the minutes, hours, days until the *Exxon Valdez* of your carnal glory runs aground in the Prince William Sound of reality and leaves your personal life awash in the thick sludge of guilt, remorse, regret, and fear.

Until then, however, you will probably have a hell of a time. Secret meetings, clandestine couplings, the high drama that makes the dullest of lives vibrate with terror and exhilaration will all be yours. You'll be surrounded with a boffer's buffet, a sumptuous array of sensual treats and sexual canapés, and you'll feel like a poor man invited to dinner at the Ritz.

Until they hand you the check.

The total will be more than you can imagine, before the tip. You'll look at the bill and say, "Wait a minute! What the hell is this?"

The sky will open and the voice of James Earl Jones will say, "This is the price of cheating."

That's when you'll slap yourself on the forehead and ask why oh why you ever poked Cynthia anyplace but in the tacky, overdecorated, red-velvet-and-black-Naugahyde bachelor pad of your heart.

WHY WE CHEAT

Thrills. Cheating, which was discovered only moments after the invention of fidelity, is what psychologists like to call "a crazy thing to do," in that not only is it self-destructive, but, clinically, it also resembles nothing so much as certain other crazy things to do, like asbestos removal and teenage drinking and driving. Think of cheating as you would, say, bungee-jumping, except let's say that the bungee's made out of old jockstraps and rubber bands and you're thirty thousand feet up in a 747 loaded with nitro and drunk Rotarians. You look down at Earth, where you were born an innocent babe and nurtured by your sainted mother, and say to yourself, "No way."

But somehow you're pulled, pushed, driven to cheating. You take the plunge. Off you go into thin air with five miles of elastic tied to your balls. Probably, on your way down, you'll realize you aren't alone on the free-fall to cheaters' hell: After all, we all know somebody who didn't want to do it, never planned on doing it, did it, and now swears he'll never do it again. Guys like that run for president.

Cheating seems a straightforward enough adventure. Two people getting together behind a third person's back isn't a very complicated mathematic. So it would seem the reasons for cheating would be similarly modest—like lust.

Instead, there are as many reasons for cheating as there are ways to cheat. Here are the Magnificent Seven of infidelity:

1. *Self-Seduction.* Often, cheating is a way to help boost a fragile but oversized ego: "I was a cheater," said Geraldo on somebody else's daytime chatfest. "It was like a drug."

Geraldo Rivera is a good example of a masturbatory cheater. Never tired of boasting to his all-female audience of his once-profligate sex life, Rivera's idea of cheating seemed to center mostly on the effect it had on him. It was, like, a drag.

Rivera, who has somehow built a sort of tabloid-level career on his ability to walk, talk, and wank at the same time, wants us to believe that cheating is an infirmity, something that must be cured, like *la grippe,* and is hence deserving of the same sympathy society extends to celebrity love addicts and celebrity crack abusers.

2. *Animal Instincts.* Here are the results of an exhaustive Modern

Man poll of American men who admit to having cheated on a wife or girlfriend: Three of them, or 30 percent, said they had been lured into cheating by the presence of an extraordinary physical condition—willowy legs, an alluring face, a pleasant smile, or, as one technician said, "big, huge tits."

Meanwhile, an amazing 50 percent said it was because they were sure they wouldn't get caught (to a man, they were wrong; see below), and that was all the thought they gave it. This sort of revel without a cause is a good illustration of why a Modern Man never leaves his girlfriend unattended and idling at the curb, metaphorically speaking.

Meanwhile, one guy, or 10 percent of the survey, said he didn't know why he had done it, or *if* he had done it, since he was too drunk to remember having done it and only *assumes* he did it because he got naked and went to bed with her wanting to do it, and woke up hoping he had, but was afraid to ask.

There is a practical application to which all this usually semiconscious conduct can be put, as a simultaneous poll of women revealed: One woman, or 25 percent of those surveyed, said she had done it in order to break up with her boyfriend. "So it wasn't really cheating," she said.

3. *Revenge.* Probe deeply enough into the dark corners of a cheater's mind, and eventually, among the scattered motives for misadventure, you'll find revenge, the global and historical basis for wars, scourges, riots, and other man-made catastrophes—including divorce. Sometimes, even the *threat* of betrayal is enough to pull the revenge trigger: "I cheated on her because I was *sure* someday she was going to cheat on me," one man said.

And did she?

"She became a lesbian." Ay-yi-yi.

This is the self-defense-before-the-fact defense. Don't try this at home, kids. Cheating as a revenge for a real or potential crime can be lethal. First of all, it establishes infidelity as a basis for power in a relationship. That's bad. Second, it results in a kind of emotional cannibalism, in which both partners hunker down over the cadaver of their romance and devour whatever affection and respect they once had for each other. Then they curse the bones.

4. *Insecurity.* Insecurity is the number two reason why people indulge in wildly promiscuous sex. (Number one is because long ago, sex used to be fun, and we're all nuts for nostalgia.)

Let's take a guy we all know, a regular Joe with a good job and a great-looking wife. We think he's okay, a normal guy. But he has low self-esteem. He thinks he's too dumb or too fat or his hair's too bozo for street use. So one day he wanders into the local bar, where the barmaid gives him a smile and a wink and a drink and a bounce on her sweet belly, *ah!* And he leaves feeling just a little less insecure—but a lot more paranoid—than when he went in.

Some people have the remarkable ability to put their own insecurities at someone else's feet. An illustration: Once, a very beautiful and semifamous actress was being interviewed by an unknown reporter who was barely average-looking. In the middle of a question about TV versus movies, she reached over, grabbed the tape recorder, pushed the stop button, and said, "Do you find me attractive?"

The reporter said, "Sure."

"Would you go out with me?" she asked.

"Well," said the reporter, "I'm married."

The actress looked crushed.

"Would you go to bed with me?" she asked.

"You bet," said the reporter.

"I'm married, too," said the actress. "So I guess that's out."

5. *Selfishness and Greed.* These two, what are you gonna do with 'em? They're the Siamese twins of bad behavior, joined at the joint and screwing in tandem. They drive an honest man to cheating because they just won't let up. They nag, nag, nag. Then they get laid. Then they want more, more! You hear me? More!

Calm that tense testosterone, you rakes and roués of Planet Earth. Don't waste your energy. Every man can be Greed incarnate, and there'll still be enough to go around. An explanation:

There are, say, 5 billion women in the world. Eliminate half because they're chronologically challenged or married to big guys. Then knock off half of the rest because maybe, like most men, you're a little choosy, you know your type, so by the time you take away all those you just *can't* screw, you're left with maybe only 1.5 percent of the total who are both available and good-looking enough to make you want to screw around on a lark. That means there are 75 million babes out there between you and China.

Now, let's say you work hard, or you get lucky, or you have the best line in the world and you score with one in ten. And let's say you live to be eighty-five and you lost your virginity when you were only fifteen (who knows, an older woman, maybe a slumming cheerleader). That means you, Mr. Median Man, can go to bed with 7.5 million women, give or take, before you die. You can screw 107,143 women a year. That's a different woman every five minutes for seventy years, no sleeping, no eating. If you wait until late adolescence to start, or if you step out for a burger, or if you die young, you might be groin-grinding every ninety seconds or so.

Now that's what an average guy can do. And you want *more?*

6. *Motive, Opportunity, and Diminished Responsibility.* This is where you're happily involved, but out of town for a convention. At a cocktail party you meet a woman from Shreveport with a little waist and big hair. You drink together all night long and stumble back to your room alone. But wouldn't you just know it? At midnight she knocks on your door. You open it and she's holding a bottle of tequila in one hand and her clothes in the other and asks if she can come in for a little, teeny chat, and you kiss her full on the lips while holding her ankles.

Is this cheating?

Yes. Motive, opportunity, diminished responsibility—all of these fragile excuses notwithstanding, ethics never sleeps.

7. *Too Much Country Music.* It just wears you down, all those women cheating on their truck-drivin' men, so you figure what the hell, might as well have a ball before the tears start to fall.

In the mobile homes of America, betrayal is a double-wide problem, old buddy, because no-good cheating men and two-timing women are part of the national myth. This is a particularly American phenomenon, but other countries have their own variations. In England, for example, men cheat on their wives by wearing their dresses, while in France, men *think* they're cheating on their wives even though they haven't quite gotten the old Arc to Triomphe for years. Instead, they smoke and talk their way through infidelity while their wives are out sleeping with the Algerian help. The clever Japanese have robots that do their cheating for them.

The point here is that cheating always seems to be a prevalent form of marital variation because it comes wrapped up in the attractive cultural paraphernalia of the moment and the place. But in fact, cheating's a dangerous pastime everywhere, and it can get you in just as much trouble in Savannah as it can in Suez.

HELPING HER CHEAT

Let's say you're a guy helping somebody else's wife or girlfriend commit a little bedroom betrayal. The cheater's accomplice gets a sort of free ride. He gets all the juice of faraway trysts or local supermarket encounters. He is the victor in a very small war. Is there a sweeter salve for a bruised ego than to have a woman risk her personal happiness, her reputation, and possibly her fortune so she can be with *you* instead of *him?*

But you realize, of course, that if she'll cheat on him, she'll certainly cheat on you. And you recognize that the oil slick of shame will cover you as well as her. And you know that her guilt is as contagious as a Hong Kong flu. You know all that, but nothing will stop you, right?

Well, consider:

THE BROTHERHOOD OF MEN

Men live in a universe of rules. Where women have mastered the nuances of situational ethics, where every circumstance comes complete with a moral logic all its own, for most men, life is like baseball: Whether the game's played in Duluth or Dallas, fair is fair, foul is foul, three strikes, etc. Men who play life without following the rules are despised by other men.

Rules don't stop men from cheating, of course. Life's filled with Hall of Famers who can, and do, toss a spitter. No, what a constant awareness of the rules of the game does is make the difference between right and wrong a little more apparent to men than to women—an observation that may require some explanation.

So. A woman might find herself involved in an affair and never understand how she got there. She meets a guy at a real estate seminar, they have lunch and check into a motel. "It just happened," she says to her friends, who nod understandingly. She may really believe it was a kind of fluke, like getting hit by a falling piano, and that there is just no logical explanation for what happened.

But in reality, she knew before the salads disappeared that she was going to go to bed with him. *She knew it at a precise moment,* after he said or did a specific thing, a thing she'll remember for years. And what happened wasn't a warp in the cosmic fabric, it was a simple case of making a decision to cheat, then cheating. What made it seem paranormal was the almost total absence of objective ethical context.

For men, however, the elements of an encounter are more clear. A guy meets a woman at a real estate seminar. They have lunch and check into a motel. But the time between the lunch and the check-in has been filled with signals and reactions, doubts, queries, and reaffirmations. By the time they get to the motel, he has made a well-defined decision that involved a rather fully articulated accounting of benefits and risks, including:

THE THREAT OF GIANT HUSBANDS

This is the enforcement branch of the brotherhood of men. There isn't much we can add to this subject—a menacing, giant husband is not a subtle problem, after all—but suffice it to say that sensible men know there is no way to judge the size of the husband by looking at the wife, and they act accordingly.

CALCULATING THE RISK

So, is it a given that cheating is not an enterprise to be undertaken lightly? A number of factors must be considered before you throw aside loyalty and honor for a quick dick-duck.

Make an Appraisal

Percentages. Let's say that no matter what, there will always be a possibility—from 1 percent to a 100 percent dead-cert—you'll get caught cheating. Remember how we used to evaluate women on a 1-to-10 scale before we learned not to objectify them as sexual objects and started regarding them as spiritual kin with intellectual worth all their own? Well, instead of giving the object of your deceitful desire a simple 1-to-10 rating, estimate her desirability on a 1-to-100 percent factor of being discovered. For example, if Teri Garr came to your house disguised as a Domino's deliveryperson—you never know—and seemed determined to make you into a philanderer, would you let her get nasty if it meant there was a 90 percent chance you'd get caught? A fifty-fifty proposition? A 20 percent long shot? Okay, so let's say Teri Garr is a 20. Now, what is Madonna? And, while we're at it, what the hell is Michael Jackson?

This handy rule of thumb—*the Percentage Risk Rule,* we'll call it—is a useful device to take with you on your infidelity forages. Most women will score in the low teens, some in the 20s or 30s, and that very rare few in the high 50s. That's if your cheating is to take place in your heart. If you plan on cheating in the cold light of reality, though, you might want to subtract 100 from each score.

Figured it out yet? Here's a hint:

YOU'LL NEVER GET AWAY WITH IT

Sorry. It's impossible. Sooner or later you'll be found out. Guaranteed. The world of cheaters is a tiny planet the size of a glass eye, where everybody knows everybody else. Think about it for a second. Can you think of *even one person in the entire history of man on Earth* who has successfully hidden his infidelity from *everyone?*

See?

I think it was Henry Beard who once developed a theory to accommodate this truth. He called it:

The Three-to-Mao Theory

And, as theories go, it's an elegant thing, with only a few moving parts and a brilliant simplicity of design. Here it is:

> *Everybody knows somebody*
> *who knows somebody*
> *who knows somebody*
> *who knew Mao.*

In other words, if you cheat on your girlfriend while you're skiing in the Andes, word will get back to her via just three unfortunately apt phone calls, and you can find yourself dumped before your last *schuss.*

YOU DID IT ANYWAY

Why do we waste our breath? After all this, after all our warnings, all our tender advice, all our concern for your best interests, you did it anyway. You bonked Cynthia one night and now you're on the run from both reality *and* fantasy.

You're on a road with many forks.

Choice One: Dump Cynthia

Let's assume you aren't going to run away with Cynthia, who, you now realize, was nothing but a passing interest anyway. Instead, you've decided you now want to go back to your sweet baby's arms. What are you going to do?

As you already know, there are only three ways to handle this situation:

• One way is, you can *lie.* If you lie, you spare your partner from a great deal of pain—but at a measurable cost to yourself. You will be filled with guilt and remorse—or maybe with the fear of being caught. You will want to spill the beans, tell all, swear never again, then be forgiven and hope the whole thing will somehow be forgotten.

No deal; it never works that way. So if you're afraid of facing the consequences, when the truth begins peeking out from around the corners of your life, *lie.* Swear it never happened. Convince your lover it never happened. Convince yourself it never happened. If you can, convince Cynthia it never happened.

The bad side: Ulcers for you, and a lifetime of Cynthia lurking in your future. Also, there's the problem of filing Chapter 11 for your morals.

The good side: No fuss, no muss, at least for the moment.

• The second way to handle the situation, assuming you really want to be rid of Cynthia, is to *tell the truth.* Once the truth is told, Cynthia becomes history, for the bond between two cheaters is the secret.

Why? Sometimes, according to a Pennsylvania Episcopalian, an apparently uncomplicated affair will develop into a near-Fatal Attraction-style complex of interwoven fears and demands. Other times, the affair will be something you wish had never happened, but now seems to be well on its way to becoming an intrusive part of your life. Or maybe the girl with whom you cheated just couldn't take a joke and is now hot on your heels, anxious to build a rosy future for the two of you.

But once you break the illicit link that binds you to the Cynthia of your life—that is, once you spill the beans—you're in the clear again. So if you really never want to see Cynthia again, tell your wife or girlfriend all about it and beg for mercy.

The bad side: Inflicting pain on your wife, sacrificing your credibility, harming your family, infuriating Cynthia.

The good side: You're now free to pursue an endless assortment of exotic romances through the Byzantine passages and medina alleyways of your heart. So, imagine a door behind which is a band of naked ukulele-playing Hawaiian harlots dancing around a pig with an apple in its mouth, and rubbing poi on their breasts. . . .

• The third and most complicated way to work this out is to *combine the elements of one and two.* That is, lie to your wife, but make Cynthia think you're having an affair with someone else.

Choice Two: Keep Cynthia

This is the conventional obverse of choice one, except here you use your affair with Cynthia as grounds for breaking off your existing relationship.

You leave huge hints around the house, variations on the old lipstick-on-the-collar routine, but with a real toxic edge—say Cynthia's minuscule underwear in your back pocket, or maybe even Cynthia her own self hiding in the closet. Pretty soon, your wife or girlfriend suspects something's up and says, "Either you get that woman out of the closet, or I'm leaving." (A more unpleasant variation: ". . . or *you're* leaving.")

For months, even years, maybe, you've been trying to figure out a way to get out of that old lackluster romance and into something a little sportier, and now the hard work's been done for you. You're a free man, except for the Cynthia thing, and you're on your own again.

What's wrong with this picture? Well, aside from the fact that resorting to betrayal in order to make your feelings known is a mite less than manly, and aside from the irresponsible health risk of overlapping sleeping partners, now you've got a real enemy on your hands, somebody who not only hates you with a passion, but who also knows you very well, and knows *exactly* how to make you pay and pay for your clumsy attempt at liberation, or whatever you call it.

Any artisan will tell you to *use the right tool for the job,* and ending an undesired relationship by cheating is somewhat analogous to performing prostate surgery with a screwdriver. Allegorically speaking, your own tool is designed for penetrating, not for prying, so using faithlessness as a means for achieving happiness is not a very craftsmanlike thing to do.

Choice Three: Keep 'em Both

No can do, big guy. If you want a high-stress, high-risk life, better you get paid for it: Move to Beirut and open a ribs place.

Cheat with One Woman Long Enough and She Gets to Wear Mistress Stripes. Mistresses occupy a venerable position in social history, of course. In the past, when rich guys lived on one planet and everybody else lived someplace else, mistresses were the more or less natural consequence of men's polygamous instinct, in which the man who could afford more than one wife took on as many as he could until he was brought to an equitable and acceptable level of personal penury.

For the rest of us, mistresses are a conceit that provides many happy thoughts. Poor men like the idea of a mistress because it reeks of sensual indulgence, in the manner of deep shag carpeting in a van. Rich guys—who are most likely to attempt to realize this quintessential bourgeois fantasy—like the idea, because it makes their dicks feel bigger than their brains. Consequently, divorce lawyers like the idea of a mistress most of all—provided, of course, that she belongs to neither the lawyer nor his client.

Alas, the bitter truth about mistresses is that virtually every single one of them wants to replace in law the woman they've already replaced in deed—perhaps out of pride, perhaps because money follows the law.

Choice Four: Dump 'em Both

Good idea? Maybe, except for one thing: If you don't have a relationship with *somebody,* you can't even *think* about cheating with *anybody.* What fun's that?

CHAPTER SEVEN

WHY WE FIGHT: FEMINISM AND THE INVISIBLE MAN

My dear young fellows, jack up the volume on that Hendrix cassette, and we'll chat for a while about what, from a man's point of view, were feminism's golden years, 1966 to 1972.

For you boys too young to recall, those six years marking the birth of latter-day feminism were the best six years to be young, single, and male in the history of the world, since not only were there an unparalleled number of young, unsupervised women around—living in dorms, sharing apartments, starting vegetarian communes—but there was also a surplus of marijuana, some pretty good music, and a red-hot sexual revolution.

Reborn feminists were at the barricades of the sexual revolution, and not a few of us stouthearted young men were right behind them every inch of the way. After a hard day at the demo, you'd gladly listen to three hours of the Marxist-feminist party line, because when it was over, the sexual revolution part would begin, and, generally speaking, you knew it would be well worth the wait. Besides, feminism, like many social movements of the time, was preoccupied with the fundamentals of a genuine issue—fair play for women—and, despite the movement's often stupefying rhetoric, most people, including most young men, were interested in seeing that the right thing got done.

Which is why, twenty, twenty-five years ago, virtually every thoughtful female in America considered herself a feminist, so obvious were society's failures in meeting the requirements of the nation's largest-ever army of well-educated women.

THAT WAS THEN; THIS IS NOW

Now it seems as if nobody wants to be pigeonholed as a feminist. Despite a decade of almost ceaseless media propaganda, poll after poll shows that even though American women still feel they must deal with a great deal of unfairness, they are adamant in their refusal to embrace the feminist label. Feminists say women have been hoodwinked by a tremendous backlash. Critics say organizations like the National Organization for Women, with its emphasis on problems faced by single, young, white women, simply don't have much to do with the problems most women face. The numbers agree: After more than two decades of nonstop recruiting, after the Clarence and Anita Show, after the Year of the Woman and Hillary and all that, NOW has only 280,000 members—fewer members than the Future Homemakers of America, fewer members than the National Association of Garden Clubs. There are more women who subscribe to *Playboy* than there are members of NOW. It's all show business: In America, feminism's a TV show, where the media—and young women in the media are NOW's most energetic supporters—trot out the local NOW spokesperson to articulate the concerns and views of all American women.*

Normally this sort of thing—women arguing among themselves—is something a Modern Man can avoid altogether. But these aren't normal times. Conflict is in the air, and a guy's got to breathe. And besides, as we shall see, we have only ourselves to blame.

*We discourage the growth of organizations like NOW at some peril, however. There are hundreds, perhaps thousands of Women's Studies majors in this country, and they all need jobs, bless 'em. The prospect of gangs of angry, unemployed feminists roaming the streets is worrying.

A FABLE

This is a fable that takes place one Tuesday night, with nothing much doing, just you and the sweetheart of your dreams and a TV set, when there's a sudden outbreak of hostility from an unexpected quarter. The subject seems to be the remote control. Television remote control units are an incredible labor-saving device, not just for TV addicts, of course, but also for hurried writers looking for a little cheap symbolism, insofar as they focus conflict so efficiently.

To you, the cable system is a talking salad bar. You graze, lingering just long enough on each channel to reduce inane sitcoms to poetic soundbites, and if you see or hear something that annoys you, you don't just push the button and change the channel—you finger the remote as if it were a phaser. You aim at the talking head and blast it, obliterate it, send it into ether. Call it crazy, but that's you, and to you, that's what a remote is all about.

Anyway, on the TV, she looks at him, he looks at her, they move to kiss, and the next thing your companion sees is Rick Sutcliffe grabbing his cup and looking in for the sign.

Inevitably, a sullen scuffle breaks out in the darkness. The issue to you is remote control control, nothing more. But the issue to her is power, and before you can say "Boy howdy" to the Cowboy Channel, you're enmeshed in a struggle with global implications, and she's packing to leave.

Let Her Go. Wait, you say, there's been a recession around here some-place, she's making more than me, I'm unhappy, too, and besides, it was a lousy night for TV. Sure, sure. But it's a fable, remember? A metaphor-ical little tale, you see, in which you sit in for all men, she represents all women, and the living room is the USA.

For a long time, but especially during the last year or two, men and women have all been screaming at each other like a zillion Ma and Pa Kettles. Meanwhile:

- The house is falling down,
- the kids are a sight,
- the next-door neighbors are selling crack,
- some lunatic is shooting through the window, and
- we're all broke, flat broke.

Once, sex was fun. Now it's politics. In chaos like this, who can discuss complex issues like education, abortion, poverty? Who's got the remote? How do we turn it all down? How do we start figuring out how to fix the leaky roof, and stop yelling about the rain?

Just when the enormity of all this finally dawns on you, your honey-pie reaches down and plugs you square in the mug with a faceful of Faludi, the inventor of *Backlash: The Undeclared War Against American Women.* Which means the dialogue you should be having about TV, the culture, technology, tolerance, and differing tastes will instead be a noisy affair in which a dissonant Faludi melody will be bashed out on the household marimbas. Susan Faludi is the latest feminist heroine, and her enterprise, *Backlash,* is the last word in angry-young-woman journalism, and, for our purposes, a handy schematic of youthful feminism's world-view.

MALL FEMINISM

Backlash considers that there is an intricate conspiracy woven by TV producers, moviemakers, hairdressers, blue jeans manufacturers, cosmetologists, and *Newsweek* editors to roll back the tremendous gains of feminism. *Backlash* is therefore not just another volume of *Oprah*-filler, it's also the latest thing in a long line of feminine products designed to appeal to the unhappiness felt by young, single, college-educated white women. If you want to see how hopelessly middle-class the rebellious feminism of the sixties has become, read *Backlash.* Faludi feminism is not the feminism of the streets. It's the feminism of the mall, a bourgeois, nicely dressed, neatly coiffed, media-savvy feminism uncluttered with children, poverty, or committed romance. Instead, it's obsessed with the annoyances of an uncomplicated life, where commitment is the cat.

Susan Faludi herself is a pretty, white, college-educated, single woman in her early thirties who once won a Pulitzer that some critics claim was based in part on another journalist's reporting. Her concern is the status of women, so clearly she has a few things to worry about, what with the widespread impoverishment of single mothers and the alarming plight of their children. But her concerns are different. She's worried that not enough women graduating from law school will be offered law firm partnerships. She's up late trying to figure out why women aren't anchoring the "CBS Evening News." She's mad about the portrayal of women as "pronatal" heroines on TV shows. And she can't believe that magazines claimed there aren't a lot of good, single men around. She knows it all has something to do with Clairol ads and sexy clothing and women who breast-feed babies. Rats in the hamper or baby-bashing in day care centers aren't part of Faludi's world.

The Good News. The good news is that since Faludi feminism is fundamentally adolescent in its interests, your girlfriend and young women like her may eventually outgrow it. After all, imagine you could frame those grand old gestures of your own adolescent rebelliousness—your affection for Suzukis without exhaust mufflers, your reliance on a head-shave for personality definition, your stonelike insistence that electric basses were *made* to be power-strummed at full volume—as parts of a well-articulated social complaint, and you'd have the working parts for something like the collegiate feminism Faludi represents. That's what made the sixties so much fun: You could wear your briefs around your ears and say you were doing it for Laotian orphans.

The Bad News. The bad news is that even though she may outgrow it, you may have to listen to your girlfriend recite the whole book first.

BUILDING A BETTER BACKLASH

In Domestic Political Disputes, the Moral Edge Is Everything. Here are some toeholds, a little list of genuine victims of 1980s backlashes—all ignored by Faludi—which your anxious girlfriend might want to clip and use as a *Backlash* bookmark.

- The elderly.
- Black and Hispanic teenagers, especially girls.
- The mentally ill.
- The public education system.
- The poor.
- Children.

SMOKE AND MIRRORS

The reason we're picking on Susan Faludi here is that if your next-door neighbors were inviting all their hoodlum friends over for a beer-bash on a school night, Susan Faludi would be the drunk girl yelling Patti Smith lyrics through the Peavey amp in the corner. Besides, she's gotten rich off her backlash thing at our expense, since for most of us, books like *Backlash* only raise the volume of what might be reasonable conversation to distortion levels, complete with screeching feedback. Plus, her attacks on her opponents have been vicious and personal, sometimes involving interview-ambushes that might be embarrassing even to other journalists. Admittedly, we're dealing in a sorely limited universe here: *Backlash* is to fashionable feminist politics what Ricardo Montalban is to Fernando Lamas.

WELCOME TO REAL LIFE

The stuff that makes your girlfriend mad at you usually isn't part of a personally felt political program.* She gets mad at you because you piss her off. Because life sucks. Because there's no soy sauce on the premises. Because you didn't flush, *plus* you left the lid up. The rhetoric she uses, the why-are-all-men-beasts buttresses to her argument, are annoying, that's for sure.

The problem is that many issues—including those with a gender focus, such as rape or the rapid spiral of numbers of impoverished single mothers—have been trivialized, gutted, or swallowed by the noise of empty rhetoric. We too seldom talk about these things in America, because there's just too much shouting going on.

In a more enlightened age, where intellectual rigor and insight might live, social movements have a way of ensuring balance. Among clever people—like Betty Friedan, for instance—rhetoric passes into debate. Debate produces theory, theory informs strategy, and, perhaps eventually, strategy yields policy. Unhappily, in America in the 1990s, we can only hear the loudest among us, so all we hear is the rhetoric.

But rhetoric is nothing more than clichés at full volume, and clichés exist because they are useful in conveying facts. Somewhere, barely audible beneath most rhetorical racket, lives a tiny buzz of quiet truth: *All this woman trouble is our fault.* Here's why:

*Even if it were, it wouldn't always help, since some men just don't know how to relate to feminism. For those guys, here's a list of the five best-looking feminists: Naomi Wolf, Catharine MacKinnon, Gloria Steinem, Patricia Ireland, and Anita Hill.

MEN'S MOVEMENT

Men Walk. Men like to whine and complain about the women's movement. Gives us something to talk about and makes us feel concerned. But much of the blame for what has transpired between men and women has to be laid at the odoriferous feet of men themselves.

Quite simply, men, in an unprecedented number, have decided to trash their traditional roles and ignore traditional masculine virtues. From a man's point of view, one appealing side of the early years of the women's movement was the idea that men's traditional responsibilities were suddenly going to be shared. It didn't take long for that liberating concept to evolve to a much higher level: Within the space of a decade, many men became convinced they had no responsibilities at all.

What Gave Us that Idea? First, we started confusing guiltless sex with irresponsible sex. Then we found that women, in seeking justification and support for abandoning *their* traditional roles, were helping to shift the moral weight in society, until we found, with great relief, that we had been very wrong in trying to support our wives and children, when what we should have been doing was letting our wives share in the glorious rewards of hard work—and using the extra money to buy ourselves Mazdas and stereos. These days, aside from those annoying Asian immigrants, not one man in twenty would dream of working two jobs just so his wife could stay home with their children, and certainly expecting a lower living standard—a smaller house, no Club Med, a *used* BMW—is out of the question. It took us almost three decades, but we finally have seen the error of our ways. Now we demand that women meet our responsibilities for us.* This is true of virtually all American men, includ-

*This is suddenly seen as a global phenomenon, incidentally, with new studies showing that women work more than men in virtually every country in the world (with the ironic exceptions of the U.S. and that other bastion of chauvinism, Australia). This isn't news. No matter how you tabulate it, a woman with a child works harder than a man every time—here, there, everywhere—and she always has.

ing many black American men—men whose widespread avoidance of civic and personal responsibilities (for whatever reasons, justified or not) has left whole communities dangerous, ruined places where women and children are in great peril.

Carry That Kid. The symptoms of what Christopher Lasch calls an "abdication" of manhood are widespread. Look, for example, at the bizarre contests waged in the contentious arena of child support. Most divorced men with kids *routinely* avoid paying for their children's upbringing: Only a quarter of all divorced men pay their full share of child support. Some duck their bills because their ex-wives defy court-imposed visitation and custody orders, and they find that with the courts generally refusing to enforce these orders, withholding payments is their only leverage. The fact that it's the kid who ends up footing the cost of this sort of conflict is often overlooked. Many men are simply greedy. Pain, greed, and revenge are motives that all men ought to ensure excludes their children. The inescapable truth: *Providing for a child is always a father's responsibility,* no matter how irresponsible, how crazy, how wicked the child's mother may be.

Remember? Trustworthy, Loyal, Helpful, Friendly, Courteous, Kind . . . The fact that some men embrace neither these virtues nor many of our other masculine responsibilities—providing for our families, protecting women and children, seeing women get a fair shake at work, giving them a little old-fashioned respect—has left many women with a world of anger and nobody to give it to, except you and me.

Feminists capitalize on this anger, but do nothing to solve the problems that cause it. They can't. But we can. For the fact is, if women are pissed off these days, we have nobody to blame but ourselves.

OK. CAN WE TALK?

Um, about that remote control issue.
   Maybe she's right.
   Maybe not.
   Here's how to find out:

- Sit on the sofa, with your girlfriend on one side and you on the other, and the TV on.
- Place the remote approximately halfway between you.
- Take her thumb and your thumb and place them both on the button marked "Power/Off."
- Press.

CHAPTER EIGHT

MODERN MISERY

So. Broken up with your sweetie, right? And now you're broken down on the highway of the heart, yes? That wide road that you thought would take you to heaven turned out to be the New Jersey Turnpike. Worse, the skyline you see up ahead is the emotional equivalent of Philly.

You trusted all your instincts, and thought you knew right where you were going. But you took a wrong turn someplace along the way, then you got lost, confused, and now you're worried that you might become the inconvenience in Room 25 at a Holiday Inn someplace outside Camden, Bob Barker on the box, and a little note pinned to your shirt.

Pick up your pants, pal. We're going to get you out of this one alive.

YOUR BASIC YIN AND YOUR FUNDAMENTAL YANG

The world of heartbreak has two hemispheres. The good neighbor hemisphere is where you live, provided you break up with her. Because the Modern Man is an encyclopedic kind of guy, devoted to covering the whole waterfront of thought on any given subject, we'll go ahead and address the notion of what to do if you break up with her. But let's be square here: If you broke up with her, you probably don't think you need our help.

It's the unfortunate denizens—shall we say the Great Unrequited?—of the other half that need a little fraternal chin-lifting.

So, first:

IF YOU BREAK UP WITH HER

Here, quick. Read this before you charge through another china shop of the heart:

Be Scrupulously Honest. Think clearly about what you're doing. You'll be giving a hard time to somebody who was once your best friend and greatest ally, so give her your best explanation of why you're breaking it off.

Be Specific. Hence, saying "I guess it just didn't work out" is not only intellectually bankrupt, it's emotionally cruel. Don't leave the responsibility for the breakup in midair. There are specific reasons for doing what you're doing. Take the time to get them clear to yourself before you retail them to your soon-to-be ex. Nothing will ease her pain so much as a concrete set of reasons why it just didn't work out.

Be Final. Breaking up is crossing the line; it's not a hazy, ambivalent kind of thing. When you say it's over, you must mean it.

If you end it on Friday, don't try to be friends again on Monday. Knock off those daily phone calls. Get out of her life. Do nothing that might possibly be construed as a gesture of reconciliation. There'll be an opportunity for friendship later.

IF SHE BREAKS UP WITH YOU

Now, this is why you've come to our little corner, yes? Because your love life just became a made-for-TV movie, right?

Of course, they always get it right in the movies. For example, when disaster strikes, it strikes in slow motion. The bullet slams into your shoulder and you spin about with balletic grace. The walls crumble gently, and the floor gives way beneath you as if you were being released by the carefully unfolding hands of God. Your mouth opens thoughtfully in a soundless scream. The devastation is complete, of course, but somehow the traces linger long in the memory and etch themselves in complete clarity.

Or, worse, imagine the perfect lips of the woman you love as she tells you to leave her and never return. Imagine her lower lip forming a soft pout as she says the word "good," and the sweet smile that must come with the word "bye." *That* is the slow-motion depiction of violence that makes all men want to hide their eyes.

If it seems like the movie of your breakup is one you've seen before— and especially if you've seen it recently—you've come to where the soft shoulder of sympathy lives, where the common scar of love abandoned is the mark that binds all men together. So if your emotional life has just been dumped into the landfill of love, read on for a little nonbiodegradable advice.

WHAT TO DO NEXT

Wait and Watch. The breakup will proceed according to a predictable pattern. You'll see it unfolding, and you'll sense your powerlessness. If you're not living together, she'll ask you to stop by her place some evening for a little "talk."

Stay Home. Most women have the idiotic notion that the best way to tell a boyfriend to kiss off is to do it face-to-face, and preferably on her turf. Don't fall for it; it's like being sent to the principal's office. *Under no circumstances allow yourself to be set up for one of these sucker-talks.* Nothing is more demeaning. The insane desire to inflict a premeditated, parting humiliation is one of the more despicable traits some women possess. For her, it's a cheap-shot "resolution," but there's nothing in it for you. When a woman tells you she thinks it's time you "talked," you should already have a good idea about what she wants to say. At all costs, get her to give you the bad news over the telephone. Or tell her to drop you a line sometime.

Shut Up. Once she tells you to get lost, don't waste your time in any further discussion. If the breakup is a phoner, say something curtly polite, then get off the telephone. And stay off.

You're going to be heartbroken, crazy-sad, completely without joy. And the only person who can make it better is the woman who just gave you your papers. *Don't call her* if you expect any comfort whatsoever. It won't be there, no matter how badly you need it. You're all alone, and even your best pal—the guy you *should* talk to—will be little help.

Count to 90. Your view of the relationship will flip-flop at least three times. Eventually, you will see the situation with some clarity. Make up an arbitrary timetable, if you must. Try ninety days. *Then,* if you still feel the need to communicate with her, you'll be able to do so with some dignity.

UNDERSTAND YOUR RIGHTS

When the barking dogs of the heart police jump for your throat, know your emotional rights. For the sake of some cheap alliteration, we'll call this your marital Miranda. When she starts blasting, remember:

• *You have the right to remain silent.* You don't have to answer every charge and accusation. Keep in mind that if she's initiating the breakup, she's already marshaled all her arguments far in advance, and any off-the-cuff rebuttal you might attempt will be feeble and inaccurate. And anything you say may be used against you.

• *You have the right to set the record straight.* Since remaining friends will be part of her program, exercise this right by stipulating that she must hear you out as the price of your friendship. Wait until you know what you're talking about, then let loose.

The best method of correcting the record is by writing a letter. Get down on paper all the things you've been trying to say, but which you know have never been heard. Cover all the bases, make all your points—but *don't undermine your desired effect by reducing the letter to an emotional screed.* Write the letter in white heat, if you must, but reread it a day or two later and rewrite it. Under no circumstances should you mail the letter the same day you write it. Remember, she already assumes you think she's horrible, and if you simply reinforce that impression, she'll be able to easily dismiss it. Dwell instead on broken promises, shared aspirations, essential values. If you wish to curse her with a barren life or a meaningless existence, do it in the form of a logical sequence of assertions and predictions. This letter is the last chance you'll have to deliver the perfect father-daughter lecture, so make sure you give it some thought. Women live in a world of constant emotional churn, so do what a man does best: With calm and exquisite logic—and, if you're man enough, some humor—explain the law and how she's broken it. While the letter may not have the ultimate effect of bringing her back or shattering her self-image, it will help you understand your own moral ground. After all, it's a lot easier to lose a battle like this if you're certain you're in the right.

Also remember that the value of the letter *to you* will be magnified severalfold if you are fortunate enough to have an account of its effect—rumor, gossip, maybe a sympathetic mutual friend.

• *You have the right of revenge.* But be careful here. The superseding rule of revenge is that you should always be sure the screwing you give is worth the one you're going to get. Never attempt to take revenge on someone unless you can control *all* the variables that will result from what you do.

WEAR YOUR TROUBLES ON YOUR SLEEVE

Breaking up is the hair shirt of the heart; either you give it to someone else or you wear it yourself, and once you put it on, you never take it off.

A really good, think-you're-gonna-die, never-again, I-am-worth-less-than-spilled-crude breakup is a lot like your first trip to Paris: You may forget the details, but you'll never forget the experience. Even an abundance of psychic knick-knacks and souvenirs will clutter your personal landscape for a good long time; everywhere you look there'll be something that reminds you of what's-her-name.

Here's the Yogi-ism you have to keep in mind, always: *When it's over, it's over.* Really. Not only that, but even if your romance should revive, it'll be a different beast. And the chances are, you won't be happy with what you'll have.

The Modern Man's advice here is to sublimate all your anguish with a little do-it-yourself—and keep-it-to-yourself—analysis, starting, maybe, with an attempt to answer the question that keeps nagging you: "What the hell happened?"

HERE'S WHAT HAPPENED

The quick-and-dirty explanation for why you're not rolling in your sweet baby's arms is that you stopped talking to each other—that's (a) or (b) You started taking each other for granted; or (c) One of you was afraid of commitment; or (d) One of you felt intimidated; or (e) Both of you just forgot to pay attention to what you were doing.

This list—a quick-and-dirty one, after all—can continue through Z, of course, it will still contain nothing but an alphabet soup of dishonest, less-than-satisfying explanations.

Here's what really went wrong: You were wrong about the person you chose to love: She wasn't who you thought she was.

Unbelievable, you say? Well, chum, your decision to make what you thought was the greatest emotional investment of your life was made with almost no valid information. Figure it out for yourself; it probably went something like this:

You met somebody, and on the first date, she laughed at your jokes, she looked like a logical explanation for sex, and she sang the sweet litany of your soul. By the time the second date was over, you had created a whole character for her, largely in order to explain why she was able to do all those wonderful things you thought you saw on your first date. And if your first date ended with hope, and your second date ended with faith, then along about the last two hours of your third date, you were a fool in love, praying for charity. You wanted to see just one little gesture, some tiny flicker of reciprocation. If you didn't see it, you made it up and convinced yourself that you were drawn to each other like electromagnets in a science project. So. After knowing this woman for only a few hours, you found you had entrusted her with a great deal of power over your life.

All you could do after that was hope for the best. But you forgot that you had created a wonderful opportunity for self-delusion. All those terrific attributes with which you tried to adorn her perhaps were all the wrong size, the wrong color, the wrong cut—just plain wrong. She didn't change, and neither did you. You both remained what you were when you started. You were just *wrong* about her, that's all.

THE REAL THING

Breaking up with your girlfriend is one thing; breaking up with your wife is quite another. There's a big difference between the two.

• *Don't accept substitutes.* Living together, as we discussed in the chapter devoted to cohabitation, is not the same as being married. Outside the narrow concerns of a courtroom, the distinctions are admittedly subtle, but they are profound and quite real.

You've seen this: You're living with Her Squeezeness in peace and contentment for years, and then, one morning at breakfast, you decide to get married. By lunch, you're calling lawyers and wondering what happened.

• *Nothing happened, really.* Nothing happened at all. And you both realized nothing else was going to happen, either, for you had deliberately cut off all other choices, all other possibilities. This realization of voluntary quarantine is a powerful psychological force, one that drives some men mad. Cohabitation is to marriage as peninsulas are to islands.

• *Amplification and magnitude.* In a marriage, everything bad grows to fill the available space. That means every flaw is a potentially fatal one, every silence is deafening, every habit a neurosis. Imagine sitting next to the same person on a flight to eternity, and you have the seating chart for marriage.

• *Shifts, dodges, alterations.* The permutation of one tiny personality trait is enough to throw an awkward marriage off-balance. Courtship is a long sales pitch in which a deal is spelled out with some precision. Marriage freezes the deal at a given moment in time—in fact, a contract is drawn up on the basis of the proposal—and any subsequent change in the arrangement can nullify the agreement. Did you promise work-free wife support? Then you have to come through. Did she promise kids? Then she has to deliver, if you'll pardon the pun.

• *You forgot.* You loved her, she loved you, then you spent ten, twenty years in each other's face, and you forgot all that love stuff. Just before you got to divorce court, you were taking her for granted and she was nagging you into a coma.

HOW COME IT HURTS SO BAD?

According to the science guys, men fall in love with a far greater degree of attachment than women do. It's all part of an insidious biopsychological trap.

There are very few ways to take the measure of a man—maybe his cars, or his job, or his niceness, or his money. But, as we've already seen *ad infinitum* in this little book, perhaps the most accurate way to evaluate the worth of a man—especially in these confusing times—is by how well he meets his responsibilities. In fantasy, a good woman spends her life waiting for Prince Charming. In reality, Prince Charming spends his life looking for a good woman. Women represent the center of a man's emotional life. When men fall in love, they immediately begin assembling all the lost luggage of their youth, all the instincts for protecting the cave, maybe, and all the lessons about duty and fatherhood. Before the sheets are wrinkled, men are building the house of their dreams, at least figuratively speaking. Men quite simply expect a relationship to create a life for them—or at least to infuse a life with some easily understood meaning. Men, therefore, often expect more from a relationship than a relationship can ever reasonably be expected to provide. They're space-walking, and when a romance ends, they're left drifting in darkness.

Women, on the other hand, are a little neater about all this; they've organized their emotional lives to accommodate a number of different attachments. Where men focus on only one context for love, women are busy creating pigeonholes for all the loves of their lives—their father, their sister, Mel Gibson, their damn cat. A woman's love for you is one of a number of involvements, all of which are given more or less equal weight.

Beyond that, when a woman breaks up with you, she's done a lot of careful planning. *She's ready. You're not.* You think everything's jake, when suddenly heartbreak batters down your door, runs into your living room, makes fart noises, snaps the elastic on your briefs, and gives you a cream-pie hat to wear on the way out.

HOW COME IT *DOESN'T* HURT SO BAD?

Some Breakups Are More Sad Than Painful. Let's say that the mojo went on vacation and never came back. Maybe she was just too damn sweet to toss into the street. Eventually, she'll get around to breaking up with you—but usually not until after she meets another suitor.

Don't Get Confused. And don't get mad. Be generous. Go through the motions of indignation, or whatever. After all, if she was sweet enough to keep, then she's sweet enough to humor, and she'll probably make a pretty decent friend. This sort of relationship usually has suffered from a nonfatal flaw involving some transient element—bad timing, maybe—and can come back in another, better guise. And if it doesn't, it doesn't matter.

A guy who has a sad breakup is obviously *much* luckier than a guy who has a bad breakup.

HOW TO TELL THE END IS DRAWING NIGH

When everything's going well, the end of a relationship seems far enough away to be measured in light-years.

But events in a romance on the brink can travel at hyperspeed. Let's say one day you get up in the morning, and, perhaps repeating a ritual to which you've both grown accustomed, you call her at home or at work, and let's say she seems *edgy*. You ask what's wrong and, if she's like every woman born, she says "nothing," and you know it's a lie. You can *feel* it, it's like spiritual enlightenment; like hot, wet weather; like the terrible thumb of God pressing you low and close to the earth. Suddenly, you find that every country and western hit has a special meaning, just for you.

Ten Signs of Rotting Love

Sometimes, that gruesome feeling will pass. But sometimes, it's one of those undeniable warnings on the highway of true love, a sign that says, BRIDGE OUT.

1. *Pronoun problem.* Something happens to the way history is rewritten when a relationship starts teetering. Where once both of you shared adventures of the plural personal pronoun variety, now she is the solo act in all those stories she tells that you so well remember being part of.

2. *Her friends* start treating you with pity—or contempt.

3. *Rituals.* One of the more comforting aspects of romance is the adherence to small rituals and routines. When these become secondary to her, you can assume you've become secondary, too.

4. *No sex.* This is an obvious one—no closeness, no threat, no sweat—and, as a rule, it's also the symptom of horribly disrupted communication; that is, since there is no intimacy in any other aspect of your love life, it seems inappropriate to keep togetherness tethered to the bedpost.

5. *You're sick.* Sure, maybe it's just a cold, but where once upon a time you would have been plied with chicken soup and comforted through the night, now she tells you to drink plenty of fluids and get lots of sleep, and maybe she'll call later to see how you're doing.

6. *The outlaw in-law.* Once, you were like a member of the family. Now you're an outcast, excluded from all the holidays on the domestic calendar.

7. *When even routine conversations* have a contemptuous tone, you're in trouble galore.

8. *You're on hold.* You thought everything was okay, until one day you woke up and realized you were in a tunnel. What gave you this insight? The fact that you could see light at the end of all this emotional darkness, maybe. Suddenly, the idea of a life after romance becomes part of your point of view. You may even find the idea of a breakup entering your thoughts, but never in a realistic or concrete fashion. After all, it is impossible to imagine *exactly* what the woman you love looks like leaving for the last time—until she does it.

9. *Too busy.* She'd like to see you, she says, but there are just too many other things that have to be done, and soon you realize that every opportunity for the two of you to be together has been jammed with errands, other friends, or preempted entirely. The bitter manifestation of this is when she asks for "space" (see below).

10. *She cheats.* Look, it's not a surprise. Unless you're a paranoid trooper out walking the dangerous perimeter of jealousy, your good sense all gone, you will *know,* without hesitation, when she's cheating. And you won't believe it. So if you need proof:

• *Omission's impossible* for a chatty woman when everything's going smoothly. Men often find they have spent eight hours in service to the paycheck god without experiencing a single thing of note. Men simply survive days at work. Women have entire *relationships* with days at work. They get to know their eight hours intimately; they think about every small atmospheric warp, and they need to share these observations. Women love to talk about the daily minutiae of their lives; we're talking excruciating detail, here, every minute of every day and every word of every conversation.

Consequently, when large pieces of time start going inexplicably astray, she's probably following them.

• *The defensiveness test.* Don't jump to conclusions, though. Wait until it seems obvious, then run a defensiveness test on her. There are many such tests: One good one is to get into a discussion of local restaurants, then ask her which ones she likes best for lunch. Prod a little. Watch for perspiration.

• *Sister of mercy.* She suddenly starts volunteering for everything and pointedly excludes you. Further, she'll put you over a barrel with this stuff, since these charitable acts will all be activities in which you would never, ever have an interest in participating, and hence would have no excuse for inquiring too deeply—or for making her feel guilty about not offering to include you in them.

• *Half-shod.* She comes home missing a shoe. Almost any other garment can be explained away. But a *shoe?*

• *He's so fine.* She casually describes a chap at the office in terms you recall she once used to describe you.

• *Sure, right.* She suggests that maybe *you* should go out with other people.

THE LEXICON OF LOST LOVE

Understand the language she speaks.

Friends. This insidious word, "friends," insinuates itself during a breakup when she's telling you she wants to be friends with you. What she's actually telling you is that she doesn't want to feel too guilty about the whole mess, and would you please leave without making a scene.

Person. Women, however, *do* have friends who are men. She'll tell you all about them, and you can be sure you're safe until she starts referring to them without any gender specificity. So when she vaguely mentions a "person," you can bet your bottom dollar she's talking about a man about whom she'd rather you didn't know too much. "I had lunch with *Bob*" is not the same as "I had lunch with a *person* from the office."

Insensitive. When a woman accuses you of being insensitive, it means she's unhappy with her whole life—not just the part you play in it—and she's decided to make you the villain in the piece. She'll take all her problems, cram them in your pockets and push them down your shirt, then throw you out the door.

Space. This Einsteinian notion is woman's final frontier. If a woman asks for "space," it means she doesn't like you as much as you seem to like her. Run for it. Give her so much space she feels like John Glenn.

THE LAST STRAW

Know Where Your Limits Are. Find what for you will be the last straw—the issue that for you is nonnegotiable, the deal-breaker. Tell her what it is, then stick to it. If you allow every miserable episode to become only the next-to-the-last straw, you'll have a houseful of blues and a haystack in the corner in no time.

ALMOST NOTHING WORKS

If your relationship is falling apart, *nothing you do by yourself will have any effect.* No act on your part will result in a desired response on her part. If your romance is in trouble, you both will know it, and the only thing that will make it better is if you *both* have a willingness to fix it.

. . . EXCEPT MAYBE THIS:

The only chance you'll ever have for getting your woman to walk toward you is to walk away from her. Almost certainly, nothing else will work. This is brilliant advice, by the way. Men have died to bring you this little truth. Just shrug your shoulders, say so long, tell her tomorrow's another day. Other miraculous moves—a pleading letter or a message passed through a mutual friend—have worked, of course. But success is so rare in these cases that it doesn't even show up on the statistical love chart that hangs on the wall of hell. And if one of these wimpy ploys should work, you'll just be sorry later that it did. Once you donate your testicles to romance, you never get them back.

The ploy of walking away from the whole mess has a much higher success rate. Besides, it's the only positive unilateral move you can make. And if you're only fooling yourself, that's okay, too, since by the time reality taps you on the shoulder, you'll be home free.

Don't try any fancy tricks. *No matter what, nothing you do is going to get her back,* with the possible exception of the shrug-and-walk ploy.

Remember all those women who once upon a time wanted you? And remember how you didn't want them? Remember how they whined and tried to make you jealous and tried to shame and cajole you into loving them the way they wanted to be loved? Remember how they asked, *"Why* can't you love me?" Remember thinking how none of it would ever move you, even a trace? Well, imagine if one of those long-lost admirers had simply said, "Well, sorry. Nice party. So long."

You'd still know how to look *her* up, right?

So get away, but get away with your attitude intact, because you'll need it later, when you feel weightless.

THE SECOND CALL

After you get the boot, and after you call your pal, make a quick call to your travel agent. *Get out of town.* Play Kerouac and drive across the USA. Go to London or Newark for lunch and a good hoot. Get drunk in a motel lounge or go drop in on nature. Stay away as long as you can afford to. Make friends in places you've never been before.

AFTERMATH

It takes six months or so for the smoke to clear, so keep low and close to the floor. Eventually, you'll see your way out. Here's what to do in the meantime:

• *Look at the other aspects of your life.* If your job is shaky and the IRS is getting up-close and personal and the landlord is closing in on you with a moving van, maybe you ought to solve the problems over which you actually have some control. Most of all, pay close attention to your job; remember that a man is defined by what he does, and that what you need more than anything else is a clear focus. Hard work can provide that.

• *Lean on a pal.* Call a buddy, tell him what's happened and that you need a sympathetic ear. Then lean on him like there's no tomorrow. Talk about it until there's nothing left to say. Indulge in self-pity, be a victim.

This is important, because men need to impose some sort of logical framework on a situation as emotionally chaotic as a breakup. Women stay on speaking terms with their feelings all the time, so when a romance falls apart, they've already got a perspective on the pain. If you're a man, however, you'll seek a syllogistic formula for all the confusion you feel. This takes a while, mind you, and you'll not get it right the first time.

• *Anything goes.* You're heartbroken, so ride with it. Do anything you want—cruise her house, dial her phone just to hear the ring, go to bed with her best friend—but be prepared for the consequences. Remember, *nothing* you do is going to get her back.

• *Recapitulate.* This is a meaningless exercise, but one that is irresistible. Go over the whole history of the relationship. Identify the landmark moments. Relive the great stuff. Be overwhelmed by mesmerizing insights. Comprehend the relationship between God and secular love. Come to a revolutionary new view of your attitude toward women and life. Keep it all to yourself.

• *Rebound.* Breaking up with your wife or girlfriend doesn't do much for your appearance. Despite the fact that you feel like a loser, keep up a decent facade. Looking good will help you snag a girl while you're on the rebound.

Even in your deeply distressed state, you will notice that there are essentially two types of women about: There is the one you've just lost, and then there are all the others. The reason all the others exist at a moment like this is to provide you with a fount of sympathy and ego-balm.

The first two or three women you date after a big breakup will serve to help you understand how much women dislike being with men who wear their bleeding noses on their sleeves. Women, after all, actually *avert* their eyes at traffic accidents. Go figure. So expect to suffer through several unsatisfactory dates until you regain your equilibrium. Once you are able to disguise your heartbreak, you'll be ready for the rebound romance that will make you well again.

Here's how it works. The woman you date on the rebound will give to you all that your lover has taken away. She will listen to you and cry for you. She will restore you and glorify you. She will amuse you and seduce you. She will comfort and nurture you and you will emotionally torture and abuse her, and somehow the books will all be even in the end.

THE CHRONOLOGY OF RECOVERY

Don't make unreasonable demands on your recuperative abilities. A broken romance is the emotional equivalent of dumping a Harley under a gravel truck, so expect to be laid up, so to speak, for a good, long while.

If there were heartache hospitals, this is what the recovery chart at the end of your bed would look like if you were following a normal recuperative path:

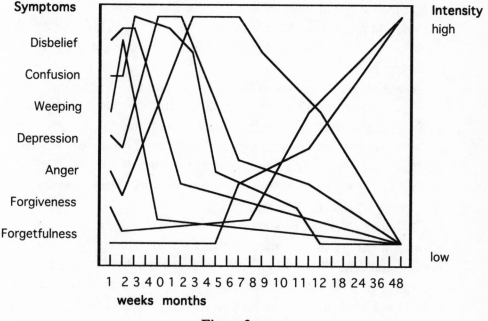

Figure 2.

NOTE: You can roughly double the duration of this chronology if you have to see your ex on a frequent basis.

• *The first day.* Don't be surprised if you experience a momentary euphoria after getting the gate. The world will look new and full of interesting challenges, and you'll immediately start thinking of women you just *know* you could have scored with if you'd only been single. Allow yourself twenty-four hours or so to return to the hard and ugly truth.

• *The first week.* As we've already noted, a breakup resembles death more than anything else—you have, after all, lost what morticians and psychologists call "a loved one"—so the first stage of postbreakup confusion will be spent in denial. For instance, the first few days will be spent waiting for her to come to her senses and call you. From the first moment you return home, you'll expect the light on the answering machine to be flashing the good news. You will check the telephone equipment you own at least a dozen times in the first week to be sure it's all working properly. At night, your friends will find you staring at the phone with the intensity of a levitating yogi. It's important to get past this stage as quickly as possible.

• *The first month* or two will be spent in endless recapitulations to friends as you try to make sense of the disaster that has befallen you. You will find yourself slipping into hours of profound sadness and grief as the reality of life without the possibility of love grows more immediate. These periodic bouts of melancholy are extremely helpful. They are a purgative of a sort—love pukes, as it were—since they represent an acceptance of what has happened.

• *The next three to six months* will be spent in trying to control a growing anger at the injustice you've suffered. The methodology of revenge and other black thoughts will occupy much of your time. It's interesting to note that this stage is a highly dynamic one, since it's difficult to maintain a high state of rage. You just sort of wear yourself out after a while.

If you have followed our advice, and if you are fortunate enough to be in a situation where she is not part of your everyday life, then:

• Sometime between *the sixth month and ninth month* you should be able to start asking yourself why it all happened. This is a question that will have plagued you from the moment she said so long, of course. The difference is that after nearly a year of upheaval and chaos and pain, only now will you begin having some answers.

• *A year or two* later, you'll wonder what all the fuss was about.

LAWYERS, GUNS, MONEY

You're going to have to deal with at least two of these three if all this heartbreak has a legal angle. *Nothing is more odious than watching a woman scramble for money* she doesn't need and doesn't deserve; it's the sort of thing that causes men to refer to women in strictly gynecological terms.

• *Children.* On the other hand, if there are children involved—*especially* if there are children involved—or if she has actually contributed to your success in a material way, then don't begrudge her a fair share. Try to keep in mind—and certainly this little book's sledgehammer reminders may help—that the most important thing a man can do is meet his responsibilities to his children. Even if she treats you unfairly during the custody skirmishes that will inevitably follow, and even if she flies in the face of the court's rules, as many women unfortunately do, remember that your responsibilities to your children are the same, no matter how horrible their mother is. In fact, your best and final revenge will be in your kids' knowledge that their papa never let them down, no matter how crazy their mama acted. Someday, one way or another, they'll tell her so—even if only by being crazy themselves.

If there aren't children involved, don't be a participant in a meaningless battle over the dog or the car or the stereo. Bail out.

• *Money for nothing.* When you figure out how much it'll cost you to be rid of her, don't forget to factor in the dollar value of having her out of your life forever.

• But above all, *don't confuse revenge and divorce* or any of its ancillary hells. By and large, divorce is payday for lawyers. You can pay her back for her sins some other, more manageable way.

THE CONSOLATION

This Only Happens Once. A devastating breakup only happens one time. If your life goes to Mars every time some woman gives you the gate, your pain isn't caused by her, but by you.

So if you can, keep it all in perspective. While it'll still be no fun, the next time you get hung out to dry, you'll be a pro. You'll pick up your life, pile it in a box, throw it in the backseat of your car, tune in the Voice of Country Music, and drive off into the sunset.

CHAPTER NINE

AFTERMATH: THE MODERN MAN'S GUIDE TO LIFE WITH VERY SMALL MODERN WOMEN

The final topic here, dear lads, is children. But our lesson will be brief, for children are really the city limits of this book, which, after all, has been designed to bring you to this point, but no further.

So think of this as a charity chapter, provided more as a consumer service, since most Modern Men know that the almost inescapable result of hanging out with women long enough is girls.

Perhaps you've seen this cause-and-effect burlesque in the lives of one of your friends: There he was, fooling around with a woman. "It's great," he said. "No strings, no complications," as if echoing the final few shots of the great sexual revolution. Then one day he calls and says, "Help! She's gone repro on me," and bingo! he's got two women on his hands. One's large, one's not so large, but they're both a big problem because now he's outnumbered, he's awash in women. Once it was him *vs.* her. He could play for a win or play for a tie, and even though he usually ended up with a loss, it was at least a contest. Now it's him *vs. them,* so he's a loser every time.

Not only that, but where once the biggest complications in his life involved such traditional nemeses as the IRS and largemouth bass, the sudden appearance of small, home-grown women brings complexities so profoundly impenetrable, so completely beyond our comprehension, that events quickly spin out of control. For children are part of the giant tumult of nature, and once you let them into your house, you become a citizen of Wild Kingdom.

Fortunately, nature has a peculiar bias toward empiricism. So look around. Someplace buried under a sea of Fisher-Price extruded plastic is:

THE LOWDOWN ON KIDS

You're bigger than they are.

Maybe not smarter, almost certainly not cuter. But bigger, and bigger's better, at least for our purposes. Furthermore, not only are we bigger than our babies, we can talk faster and we can come up with better excuses for screwing around. So we get a lot of latitude—or at least enough latitude to manufacture a set of options.

CHOICE

There are basically two ways for a man to go when it comes to raising kids.

Old-Style. The way old-timers did it was to concentrate on being a good provider. This means taking on gender burden big-time—and these days, that's not approved, not stylish, not parentally correct.

New-Style. The other way is to proceed with your life relatively unfettered by the incessant, usually unreasonable demands of kids by simply putting your own concerns ahead of theirs. This choice is fashionable, contemporary, and very, very correct. It's the approved style of parenting most familiar to anybody not in a coma in modern America: It's parenting as seen on TV, in the White House, in the movies, and anywhere else the postwar generation celebrates itself.

These two approaches, of course, constitute what we in the pontification business like to call *The Big Issue,* since they mirror the larger choice every generation gets to make: *Either society is devoted to the nurturing and welfare of children, or it's devoted to the gratification of adults.* These are mutually exclusive concerns; children are so damned intrusive and demanding that you can't have it both ways.

Most guys take one look at this little menu and say there's really no choice. You chose the old-fangled way, you're supporting a whole family all by yourself. Choose the other, newer way, and you've got a problem with sibling rivalry, maybe, what with inner children squabbling with outer ones. But at least you've still got a life. And after all, if our children really loved us, they wouldn't want us to be unhappy, would they?

IF THIS ISN'T FOR YOU . . .

You have a big problem, because raising children the old-fashioned, unapproved way is a headache. You'll get no help from anybody, and grief from everybody; your life with your wife as a couple will be considerably more lonely, and you'll be out of step with the rest of middle-class America. Plus, you'll give up enormous amounts of time and energy to an ungrateful tad, and one of you—and it'll probably be your wife, who may forever use it against you—will have to put a job or a career on hold while the kid grows up. For that, she'll be reviled by other, more progressive-minded women. And, finally, you'll be living on a fraction of your former, two-job income.

And what's in it for you? Wrong question, but the answer is nothing, really, except the vague satisfaction that comes from doing the right thing and realizing that fatherhood is where all manly responsibilities begin. Mostly, the only beneficiary of this variety of child-growing is the kid. So you can look at this as a tax-deductible donation to the next generation, and that in itself will make you an oddball, since virtually the only other things our generation is going to give to the next one is a pile of bad literature, some really stupid art, and a national deficit the size of the Ritz.

If you are still undeterred, we offer herewith some cheap advice, gleaned from here and there:

STAY CLOSE TO HOME

Although not without some meltdown problems, nuclear families are fine. But extended families are much better, since the family's values and traditions are seen as part of a larger social context. Religion provides the same big picture, by the way—plus, the conveying of a religious tradition also provides a useful device for measuring self-scrutiny and youthful rebellion.

MÜNCHEN MAMAS

Risk Unpopularity. Harry Stein has pointed out that women will do anything to keep peace in the household. To a mother, conflicts over TV shows, telephone tie-ups, and toy-mongering are all just so many inconsequential, domestic Südetenlands. Hence, she will forever be Chamberlain, the appeaser. So you must forever be Churchill, the warrior.

Don't Be Mom. Alas, to any sensible kid, you're both Poland. Nevertheless, the distinction between the appeaser and the confrontationalist is one of the first and most pronounced differences to arise between mothers and fathers, since every kid knows that mothers who give in are kind and gentle, while soft-touch fathers are wimps and dweebs. Kids don't confuse a mother's care with a father's guidance.

Ironically, it's usually men who intentionally confuse these roles, often by competing with an absent mother for the family nurture award. Women never get these roles mixed up: They know very well that most moms who play dad do so not out of choice, but out of impoverishment or abandonment. Quite rightly, most would rather just be moms, if they could. On the other hand, dads who play mom usually find they do better when they simply try to be great dads.

Just as there's a difference between moms and dads, so there's

THE DIFFERENCE BETWEEN BOYS AND GIRLS

From a man's point of view, small boys are small men. A guy looks at his son and says, one way or another, "Been there, done that," and waits for the worst. Men understand boys with rather complete clarity; indeed, most men still see themselves as boys—a point driven home repeatedly by impatient women. To a man, his son's life is a sequence of familiar mileposts, and he finds great solace in revisiting his own youth by experiencing it again through his son. Moreover, men see themselves so clearly in their sons that the recurrence of a father's failure is cause for his outrage when he sees it again in his boy; men find it easier to measure their sons' progress in terms of missed mistakes than in terms of success, mostly because a man's mistakes are far more intrusive to him, and far more important than his successes. And besides, that's the way his old man measured him.

From a boy's point of view, of course, fathers are large devices manufactured solely to say "I told you so" repeatedly. It takes a lot of forgiveness to be a good boy. Women accuse men of oppressive paternalism; they ought to live life as a father's son. But we also know boys are merely incomplete men who only achieve wholeness when they understand that it's a father's absolute duty to provide correction and guidance—and so demonstrate love and affection—even at the risk of permanently alienating his son. Also, mothers love sons without reservation. Fathers don't.

Girls are a different story altogether. Because they are competition for women and because they are mysterious to men, most couples hope their first born child will be a boy.

For these dim lights, we offer *The Kretchmer Proclamation,* which was issued on receipt of a note from a certain Modern Man who stupidly complained when he discovered that his first child was likely to be a distaff model. "First of all, my wart-brained friend, if your number one child turns out to be a girl, you must kneel down in the direction of the sunrise and praise the gods, each and every one of them. Girls, I tell you from many years of observation (not experience, I had boys, but then again, that's experience) are the appropriate first child. They socialize the house, raise its intelligence level for the next children and solidify the family. They are loyal, perceptive, canny, and they make far better mimics than boys, therefore leading to much more humor at meal and bed times. You will mark the day I told you this."

If you, too, wish for boys, but have girls, you will mark the day you read this.

HOW TO MAKE DAUGHTERS

According to science, as hypothesized by some men and proved by others, and as received at Modern Man Central:

- *To Make a Boy Baby:* Eat junk food, stay up late, go easy on the exercise, and make love like a beagle.
- *To Make a Girl Baby:* Eat a carefully balanced diet of low-fat, high-protein foods. Get plenty of rest and drink plenty of fluids. Make love like a Methodist.

CHIA POP

Daughters master their fathers so comprehensively and so effortlessly simply because everything a daughter does is surprising to her father. Invariably, a woman who is successful with men has been a successful daughter, since she has learned not only how to make herself understood to her father, but also how to make him a little less of a boy and a little more of a man.

Family Darwinism. This can be a painful lesson, of course. Put a daughter in a man's house, and pretty soon the walls are decorated with new exercises in perception, such as the schoolroom chart of the family food chain, which shows how intelligence and civility descend, Darwin-style, from the big ape who is papa through the nurturing hominid who is mama to the highly evolved being that is daughter. This view is incessantly reinforced by girls' attitude toward their dads: To them fathers are sort of like big, idiotic but lovable pets, kind of like giant hamsters who can read maps and assembly directions, and who can do heavy-lifting tricks and buy cars on command.

Daughters are often fearful of fathers, even as they are fascinated by them. This paradox can have an unfortunate effect later in life: Full-grown women can't quite get past their insatiable need to talk about men almost as much as they talk about each other. (This preoccupation is even more pronounced in latter-day feminists; hence the thousands of books by women on men, man-problems, men-beasts, father-oppressors, and so on. Men, on the other hand, are bored by a lot of talk about either men *or* women. This book is an example, since it's about twice as far as any normal guy ought to go with girl-talk.)

Happily, for the most part, daughters adore their fathers, without much undue complication. In fact, sometimes they adore them even more than they adore trolls and ponies—well, trolls, anyway. This remarkable, often undeserved affection provides one of life's most pleasant opportunities, namely:

THE REINVENTION OF THE MODERN MAN

Most daughters love most fathers completely, and for a time remain senseless to their old man's most obvious failings. Consequently, at the first sign of a daughter, a smart man will take stock of himself, ditch his feckless friends, break his evil habits, and start spackling the holes in the drywall of his soul. For the love of a daughter allows a man the only chance he'll ever have to reposition himself a little closer to perfection—while at the same time defining for a girl exactly what a man should be.

Ultimately, of course, daughters will perceive flaws in their fathers. But better they be small ones—perhaps a certain inability to toss a football, or maybe a stubborn refusal to see charm in moronic, teenage suitors—than big ones, like selfishness or stealing or hitting.

Golden Age of Dads. Once upon a time, fathers had a lot more housework to do than they do today. In their own homes, they were theologians and magistrates, sheriffs and protectors, grand wazoos of a tiny principality in which they had the last word on all matters economic, political, spiritual, legal, and educational. Today, they have even less political power than the Queen of England, in that they lack influence and most of them would rather not be consulted, especially during the news.

So Modern Men bent on renovation know better than to look at modern models. Instead, they look for the smartest man in the world, and hope he'll come up with something useful.

AT LAST! THE SMARTEST MAN IN THE WORLD SPEAKS OUT—ON FATHERING

The Smartest Man in the World, of course, was George Leinwall. Dr. Leinwall, who died January 1, 1993, was a very ancient bibliophile, a notorious curmudgeon, and an ardent Joycean who lived in Maryland, where he tended his garden and received occasional visitors with gruff regret. When a now-defunct magazine wanted to know a little something about the then-fascinating phenomenon of "fathering," an editor with a tape recorder was dispatched to gain an audience with the SMW. The following is a brief excerpt from the transcript of that interview:

• *Visiting Editor: What advice do you have on fathering?*

• *SMW:* What's "fathering?" We used to do something *like* fathering, only we called it "having kids." We weren't important enough to *father*.

The whole idea of fathering, in my mind, is symptomatic of the trouble with this generation, with these kids that grew up in the sixties. They think they're the only ones that have ever had kids, that have ever faced a father's problems. The sixties represented a real generational fracture, and unlike most previous generations, this generation for a long time has been defined *as a group*—first by pop culture, then by pop politics, then by pop psychologists, and finally by loudmouths on "Oprah" and "Donahue." People actually believe that nonsense, isn't that incredible? There's a specialist in every damned thing these days. It's ridiculous. There are a million experts out there on "fathering," and a million people want to hear what they have to say. What ever happened to the idea of a father representing authority and wisdom, instead of representing a victim, a trend, or a phenomenon?

Look: Trust yourself. Piaget, Erickson, Freud, Hall, Havighurst, and those people spouted out nonsense about things like the conflict between determinism and environmentalism and all that. But they didn't know what they were talking about. You'd think what they said was gospel. But they're just more experts. As it is, we already allow our wives—or *any* expert, really—to take the initiative in raising our children. We're insecure, unsure of what we're supposed to do as fathers, because when it comes to kids, fathers are the most adept at shrugging off responsibility.

But, like it or not, *you* are the authority figure when your child is growing up. Wait until she's twenty-five or thirty and you see her taking responsibility for her own actions because she learned what responsibility is from watching you. *Then* you'll know as much about psychology as anyone needs to know.

Once, you respected your father because he was the authority, the expert—and the breadwinner. And your mother helped instill that respect. You grandfather, or your great-grandfather, they lived in a different kind of family. They lived in families where the *family* was more important than the *individuals* in the family, where sacrifice was not exceptional, but was often essential, where there was an aura of respect and authority for mothers and for fathers. Now, children have no respect for their parents because parents have no respect for their children.

• *V.E.: So what can fathers do to regain that respect?*

SMW: Relinquish your youth. Make a gift of it to your children. That's first. Second, if you decide to have children, don't try to maintain the lifestyle of a childless couple.

• *V.E.: Isn't your view of fatherhood rather paternalistic?*

SMW: Idiot. Yes, it's paternalistic. So what? Accept the responsibility of authority. Some men will argue that it's a good thing that fathers aren't authority figures, and that it's a good thing to be pals with their children. But just as fathers aren't mothers, families aren't groups of friends. The family, in order to survive, has to have a structure, and that structure inevitably involves specific types of responsibilities for both mothers and fathers. Fathers are responsible for the protection and support of their families, and for helping to teach their children a sense of the world. This stuff isn't society's responsibility or government's responsibility. It's the responsibility of fathers. And it never goes away.

I remember my own father, who was a very dignified man. But because of his status as an immigrant, when he came here, he had to take a menial job. And I remember how every now and then he'd sadly tell my mother that he'd have to ask his boss for a little advance to meet the rent. I used to feel for him, because he had this great sense of dignity and I could feel how degrading it must have been to him to have to ask for help.

But would my father have ever said to my mother, "Get a job?" No, *no.* It was *impossible:* There were kids at home. I can't imagine my father accepting the *shame* of it, the shame of not meeting his responsibilities, the shame of people saying, "He can't support his family." The *shame.*

So answer me this: What ever happened to that shame?

At which point the Smartest Man drew his interview to a close, as we do now this little book.

Notice

All sensible Modern Men welcome a little modern advice from time to time. If you have comments, queries, or suggestions, please get in touch and we'll put you on our modern mailing list. The address:

Modern Man
P.O. Box 26
Clearville, PA 15535-0026

ACKNOWLEDGMENTS

Like *The Modern Man's Guide to Life,* the book which preceded this one, *The Modern Man's Guide to Modern Women* has been shaped from the Silly Putty of real life. However, unlike the technique used in the *The Modern Man's Guide to Life,* where most of the contributors were acknowledged by name, here the majority of the men and women—the so-called "bunch of other guys" touted on the title page of the previous book—who allowed themselves to be interviewed on the subject of massive romantic failures and marginal accomplishments preferred to remain nameless, to such an extent that naming those who didn't want anonymity would have been awkward for the rest. So, in all cases, I salute you, you who have already died a thousand deaths.

This book is based almost entirely on the "Thinking Man's" series of articles written for *Playboy* magazine. Hence, profound thanks are proffered here to Arthur Kretchmer and Peter Moore, to the first for commissioning the pieces in the first place and to the second for rendering them into readable English. By virtue of its origin, much of this book is aimed at young, single men, perhaps the sort of lads who emerge, blinking, from modern university orientation seminars in which it is explained to them that they are all already rapists, but are too insensitive to know it. To these guys, I can say only that this is a noisy age in which most conversation between men has been drowned in a blood-dark sea of ill-formed self-righteousness. I hope this modest book, filled with little lessons gleaned from many men and women, will keep you engaged until the din subsides. And I thank you for buying a copy.

I also thank the league of flat-eared fellows—notably Stanley Bing, Bob Dattila, Barry Golson, David Hirshey, Mike Lafavore, George Leinwall, Guy Martin, P. J. O'Rourke, Steve Randall, Steve Slon, Harry Stein, Gene Stone, Gregg Stebben, Fred Schruers, and Al Wellikoff— who often spent too much time on the telephone listening to the likes of me prattle on about wimmen. I ruthlessly used their idle observations and casual chitchat in ways they never would have imagined (and certainly in ways they may find at odds with their own views). Also, as he did with *The Modern Man's Guide to Life,* Alan Rose contributed time and effort to this book, making several valuable suggestions.

Most of my sources were men. But to the co-authors of *The Modern Woman's Guide to Life*—Elizabeth Chapman, Karen Kriberney, and Maggie Kassner—and to Mary Ellen Iwata, Ellen Popiel, Mala Schein, Priscilla Turner, my wife, April, and many other generous, wise women who remain anonymous, I am also deeply obliged.

On another practical level, I really must thank Craig Nelson, Lauren Marino, Tom Cherwin, and Jenna Hull at HarperCollins for undertaking a publishing activity portions of which are wildly at variance with current political correctness.

—DENIS BOYLES

INDEX